Anthon Astrom, Dorothée Bauerle-Willert, Susanne Bieri, Christian Kern,
Felix Lehner, Claudia Mareis, Gerhard Matter, Philipp Messner, Paul Michel,
Hans Petschar, Tobias Schelling, Marina Schütz, Fabian Wegmüller,
Hans Witschi, and Lukas Zimmer / Translated by Alta L. Price

The Dynamic Library

Organizing Knowledge at the Sitterwerk—
Precedents and Possibilities

Soberscove Press
Chicago

*The Dynamic Library: Organizing Knowledge at
the Sitterwerk—Precedents and Possibilities*
presents essays in translation from the 2011
German-language publication, *Archive der
Zukunft: Neue Wissensordnungen im Sitterwerk*.

Originally published by the Sitterwerk in
St.Gallen, Switzerland, *Archive der Zukunft*
documented a symposium of the same name
held at the Sitterwerk in November 2011.

Contents

Introduction

Background

The symposium *Archives of the Future: New Orders of Knowledge at the Sitterwerk* held November 4–5, 2011, was the result of discussions about opening the art library to a broader public. Ongoing conversations with artists
suggested that new breakthroughs could be made in terms of how books
were arranged on the shelves, thanks to the use of RFID (Radio Frequency
Identification). Close contact with the material archive and art-production
practices triggered the desire to create a more flexible interface between
books and materials via digital networking.

A glimpse back into the Sitterwerk's history and surroundings fosters a
deeper understanding of the background and development of this particular
project. Felix Lehner established an art foundry in Beinwil am See in 1983,
starting out with only two employees. In 1994, the company moved into the
larger buildings of the former Sittertal textile dyeworks, on the outskirts
of St.Gallen, and today it works with approximately forty employees. The
foundry's openness to new ideas and technologies has helped it steadily
grow, and it is now a recognized center specializing in the production, as
well as restoration, of three-dimensional art works.

Parallel to its commercial work, the foundry has also launched several
noncommercial cultural initiatives, which were united under one roof in August 2006 as the Sitterwerk Foundation. Its four divisions are: the *Kunstbib-
liothek* (art library), *Werkstoffarchiv* (material archive), *Kesselhaus Josephsohn* (Josephsohn boiler-house exhibition space), and *Atelierhaus* (studio
house). The close relationship between the foundation and foundry positions Sitterwerk as a major center for art and production, a unique facility
capable of combining traditional craftsmanship with cutting-edge technologies in theory and practice.

Upon the establishment of the Sitterwerk Foundation, the art library became a publicly accessible reference library. In 2007, it joined the St.Gallen
library network (SGBN), whose database is connected to Sitterwerk's catalog, making its inventory of books and materials searchable as well. The
majority of its approximately 25,000 volumes on art, architecture, design,
and photography were part of a bequest from avid collector and connoisseur
Daniel Rohner (1948–2007), who had brought them together as his personal

library. Felix Lehner also contributed a large number of specialized books on casting technology, bronzes, restoration, and conservation from his own collection.

Right from the start, the Sitterwerk team and Daniel Rohner hotly debated how the books should be arranged. The interiors of the former textile dyeworks had been renovated, and for the first time Rohner's entire book collection could be brought together in one spot—previously, the volumes had been boxed up and stored in the attics and basements of various friends and acquaintances. The fundamental question of how to systematically organize such vast holdings was just one aspect of transforming Rohner's private book collection into a publicly accessible library. Private collections are always influenced by their creators, whose tastes and personal stories are intimately connected with the books. In Rohner's case, this involved close connections with art and artists, curators and gallery owners, booksellers and antiquarian dealers. His own highly subjective history of art determined the books' initial arrangement. He presented and explored these personal associations by setting up several groupings of books on the various tables of the art library, which in turn sparked stimulating discussions between collectors, foundry staff, and visitors.

RFID in the Art Library

As the Sitterwerk staff's own experiences and Rohner's unique vision came together, it soon became clear that the character of his private library should ideally be retained, and therefore an open, dynamic organizational system would be the best solution. The subjective knowledge of both the collector and the art library's users would be taken into consideration, and the thematic compilations created as researchers consulted the holdings would be recorded both digitally and physically, in the database, as well as on the shelves and tables. This dynamic approach allows for serendipitous discoveries, so researchers can find relevant material even in places where they didn't know to look for it. This lets readers gain knowledge for their own research, and also opens up new and surprising perspectives. All this led to the implementation of a novel solution using RFID technology, a dedicated database, and a custom-developed device to easily record each book's location. Out of respect for the book as an (ideally well-designed) object, the traditional exterior spine label was dispensed with, in favor of an RFID tag attached to the book's interior. This keeps the book's haptic nature intact, complete with all traces of light wear and tear over time.

As the RFID device makes its daily rounds of the bookshelves, its antenna reads each book's tag, so the book's current location is transmitted to the digital catalog. Inventory is taken at such brief intervals that this could be considered a permanent inventory of sorts, updated daily, allowing the books to exist in a highly dynamic, flexible order. In this sense the art library adapts to its users, who can make their own subject-specific or associative arrangements on the shelves. Another goal was to connect the two collections of the art library and material archive. The idea of using tables as Rohner did, to display groupings of books, seemed ideal. It was further developed so that each table was equipped with RFID antennas, and then the database was expanded to include a list of the books laid out on a table, so materials could be saved in thematic groups, and researchers could annotate the records with additional comments. With the user's consent, these data sets can be made available to the general public, so Sitterwerk has successfully created a platform for knowledge sharing and enhancement.

The Symposium

Although this pilot project had been decided upon, the ongoing discussion of libraries' classification and organization systems was still far from over. Librarians' attention to the matter was heightened, and speaking with researching artists and other art library users allowed them to gain insight into new options made possible by digital media and the Internet. In light of their experiences with this pilot project, and together with Zurich-based creatives Anthon Astrom, Fabian Wegmüller, and Lukas Zimmer—who at the time of the symposium were working collectively as the Café Society— library staff came up with the idea of organizing an interdisciplinary symposium on orders of classification and knowledge systems.

Further discussion led to the identification of three key focus areas— classification systems, art, and new orders of knowledge—each with three contributions. Gerhard Matter, chief librarian of Basel's cantonal library network, introduced and moderated the first portion. Susanne Bieri, a longstanding trustee and member of the Sitterwerk library's advisory board, as well as head of the graphic collections of the Swiss National Library in Bern, dealt with the field of art. The second day of the symposium explored how the dynamic order in the art library and the material archive can be a starting point for thinking about new opportunities in digital and analog applications, and what effect these might have on the future of information organization in archives.

Classification Systems

Paul Michel, emeritus professor of German literature at the University of Zurich and a renowned specialist in the history of encyclopedic knowledge, opens the first section with "Organizing Knowledge," wherein he lays out the fundamentals of historical knowledge-classification systems, while highlighting their relativity. It is enlightening, especially with regard to the supposed authority of these hierarchical systems, to recall one of Diderot's key assertions, made in his 1755 *Encyclopédie*: there are as many systems for classifying human knowledge as there are individual points of view.

Tobias Schelling, a librarian who served as a project manager at the Zentral- und Hochschulbibliothek Luzern (Central and University Library of Lucerne) in 2011, provides an overview of his experience with organizational systems in libraries and how they've changed through the centuries. He begins with a concrete example—the renovation and transfer of certain portions of the library where he works—and outlines three different organizational systems, each typical of the period in which they arose. He then offers a critical discussion of open-access systems in academic libraries: what are the benefits of open access, what are its limits, and what might the alternatives be?

Philipp Messner, cultural scholar and archivist, recalls a pioneer of applied information science in his contribution, "New Orders of Knowledge around 1900." Karl Wilhelm Bührer (1861–1917), curator of the Mittelschweizerischen Geographisch-Commerciellen Gesellschaft ("Central Swiss Geo-Commercial Society") and library assistant, considered the bound book an outdated form, because information in the form of thoughts is freely movable, easily combined, and rearranged—hence he felt card catalogs were the ideal system. This flexible, free-form approach was the only one that would make an associatively structured, individually oriented knowledge system possible. Today, thanks to comprehensive digitization, Bührer's ideas can readily be put into practice.

Art

Since the end of the twentieth century, collecting, recording, storing, and archiving have become increasingly important artistic strategies. Artists often see themselves as forensic researchers and material collectors. Looking into the past with the goal of classifying, organizing, and analyzing has become a formative element of our individual and collective memory. As Silvie Defraoui and her late partner Chérif Defraoui demonstrated in their collaborative work *Archives du futur* ("Archives of the Future," 1975), collections are repositories of knowledge with great potential.

The fluid combination of images from the past, visual memories, and their resulting insights had long been art historian Aby Warburg's (1866–1929) main subject of research. He sought to establish a comprehensive cultural science with no borders between the disciplines, which led him to develop his iconological method, thus paving the way for our modern approach to art-historical research. Warburg's transdisciplinary approach remains highly topical, as the plethora of new publications and colloquia on his work attest. Therefore, the section of this book devoted to art opens with Dorothée Bauerle-Willert's contribution on Warburg's picture atlas and cultural studies library. Warburg's mobile library and his last, unfinished project, the *Mnemosyne* picture atlas—a dynamic arrangement of individual images—created a *Denkraum*, a "space for thought," whose flexibility continuously generates new questions and insights.

Since 1989, the Swiss artist and musician Hans Witschi has lived in New York, where—impressed by the quality of American print media, especially the *New York Times*—he began to systematically collect press photographs. His rapidly growing collection of images featuring hands soon flooded beyond the confines of his sketchbook. The resulting *Handbook* is an exemplary specimen of collections' and systems' artistic applications. Witschi has experimented with both the material and haptic aspects of this work, as well as digital solutions for how to best present it. He is currently working on bringing his pictorial and other artistic work together in a complete digital archive.

Hans Petschar, director of the picture collection and graphics department at the Österreichischen Nationalbibliothek (Austrian National Library), vividly describes efforts to create a catalog for Holy Roman Emperor Joseph II's library in his contribution, "Notes on the Cataloging of Vienna's Imperial Library." He chronicles how Gottfried van Swieten, prefect of the Imperial Library in Vienna, enlisted library officials and an expanded staff of assistants to create an "organized, complete" catalog during the summer months of 1780 and 1781. The use of outside consultants meant the work had to be uniformly coordinated, so general rules were drawn up dictating how the books were to be described. Although the primary catalog (listing author and title) was completed, they never managed to complete a catalog arranged by subject. Swiss historian Johann Müller—who in 1800, against van Swieten's wishes, was named the library's first curator—wrote a letter reporting that the library's several hundred thousand volumes were not arranged in any kind of systematic order. Van Swieten was against the idea of a subject-based catalog, and argued that a purely mathematical, absolute classification of the disciplines was not possible. Much like Diderot, he believed that such designations were invariably subjective, and therefore felt it made no sense to establish any systematic order.

New Orders of Knowledge

Anthon Astrom, Fabian Wegmüller, and Lukas Zimmer also offer new possibilities for using digital media to envision systems of knowledge organization. For the past five years, these three researchers have been exploring how reading and writing on digital surfaces compares to the use of more traditional, paper-based media. They have found that most people's thought processes are still significantly shaped by classical orders of knowledge, especially the structure and culture of the book, which is considered our primary form of knowledge to date. Astrom, Wegmüller, and Zimmer came up with their own targeted projects, examining topics, such as how so-called bodies of knowledge can arise in the digital realm, and how such applications allow for new ways of representing relationship networks. Given the practical benefits of such systems, Astrom, Wegmüller, and Zimmer also organized a workshop prior to the symposium, featuring exercises relating to the Sitterwerk art library's pilot project.

Christian Kern, agronomist and owner of InfoMedis AG, has many years of experience working with RFID technology in libraries, and helped implement its use at Sitterwerk. His contribution, "RFID: Applications and Implications—A Foundation for the Internet of Things," shows how, some thirty years after its development, RFID has become a part of everyday life. It isn't widely known that RFID was first used for livestock management. Nowadays, ski areas wouldn't be economically viable without it, and even hospitals depend on it to manage patient data. In the latter part of his chapter, Kern explains the development and application of this technology at Sitterwerk.

Design researcher Claudia Mareis analyzes the humanities' growing interest in design practices and design-related issues in her contribution, "Design Research and 'Mode 2' Knowledge Production." A key step in knowledge-production and diffusion processes involves their material manifestation, be it as lecture, essay, book, archive, or patent—and because this form is physical, it must be designed. How might various forms of representation and visualization—charts, graphs, etc.—promote or inhibit the communication of knowledge? The idea of a *design turn* in cultural studies aims to bridge the gap between theory and practice. Since the latter half of the twentieth century, knowledge has been produced not only through traditional academic means (Mode 1), but also through the context of its application, now its primary form of production, which is both interdisciplinary and transdisciplinary (Mode 2). In this sense, design must play an active, formative, mediating role in interdisciplinary discourse, giving form to knowledge.

Looking Ahead

The two-day symposium brought together these speakers and an engaged audience, sparking an ongoing dialogue. The Sitterwerk will continue to broaden its network through conversations with additional partners; it considers itself a think tank of sorts, incubating innovative approaches toward knowledge and organizational systems. As Felix Lehner describes in his text, related research projects, workshops, and regular meetings are already in the works.

The catalogs of both the art library and the material archive's holdings, as well as their dynamic systems of organization, can be explored at www. sitterwerk-katalog.ch.

Marina Schütz

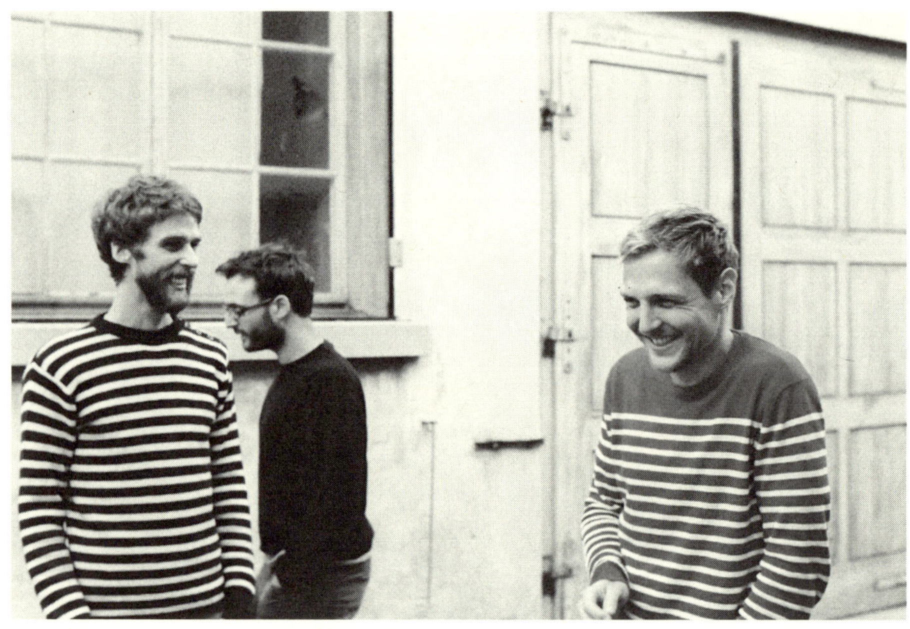

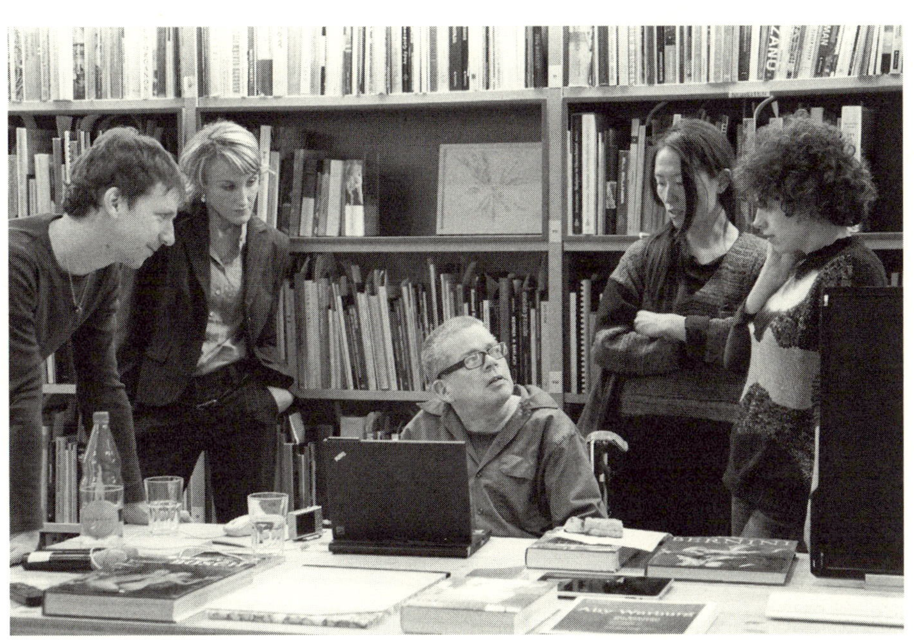

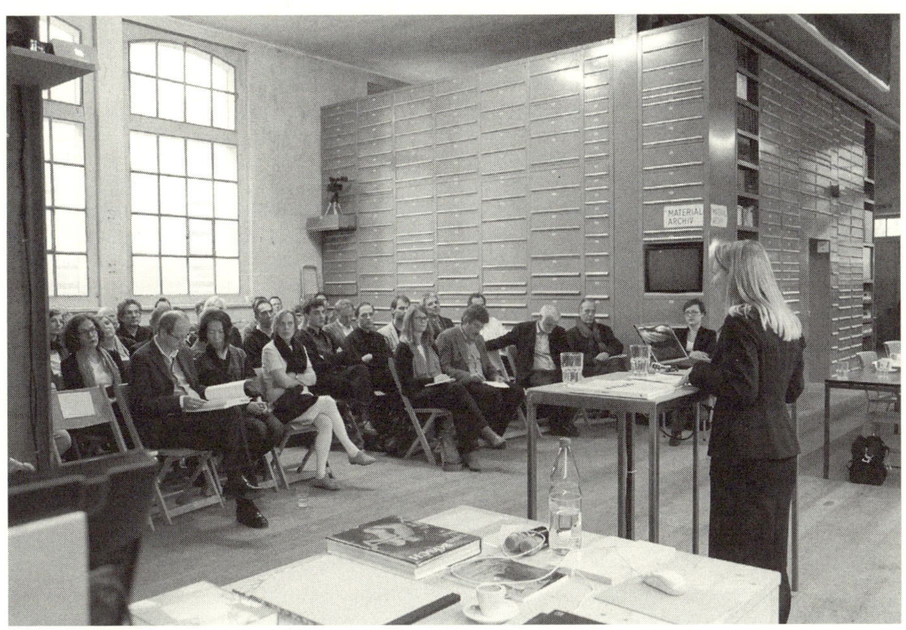

■ Anthon Astrom, Lukas Zimmer, and Fabian Wegmüller. ■ Hans Witschi, with symposium participants. ■ Susanne Bieri introducing the art division.

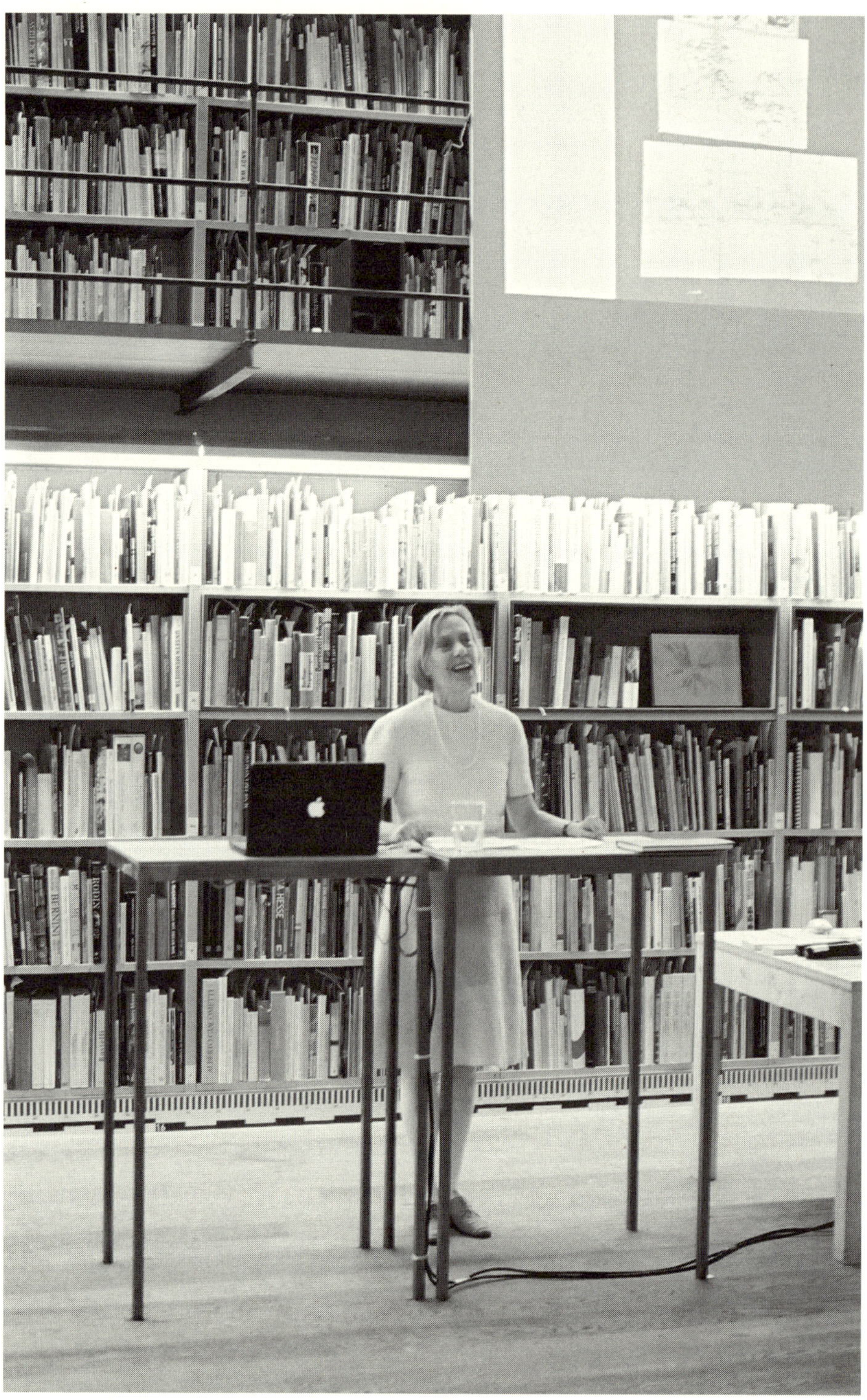

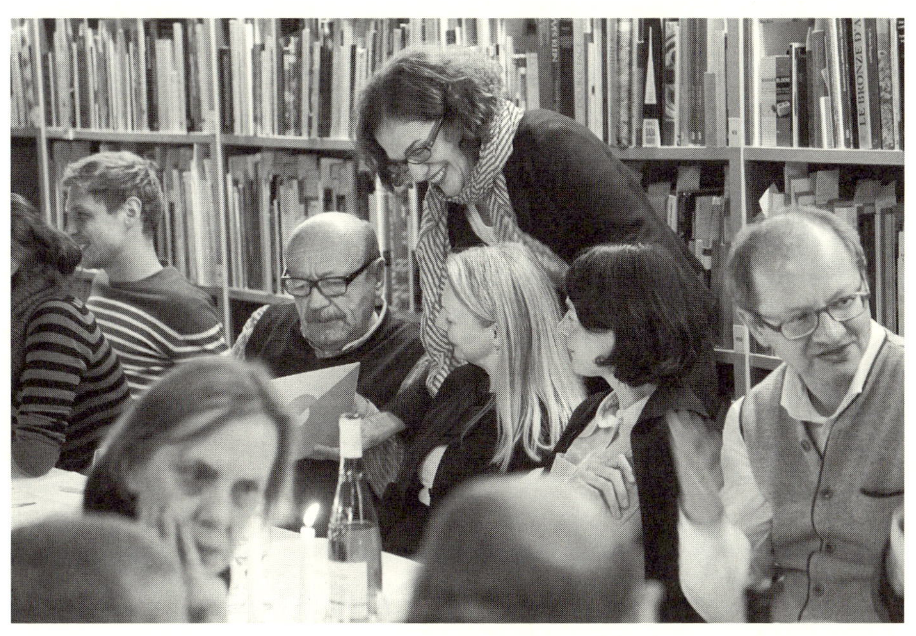

■ Dorothée Bauerle-Willert giving a presentation on Aby Warburg. ■ Participants and speakers enjoying dinner in the library.

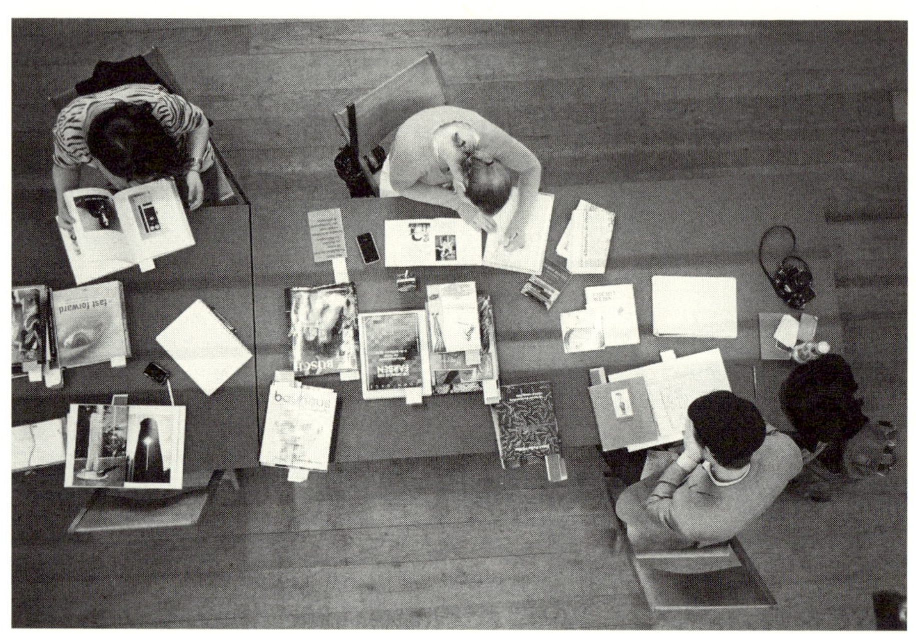

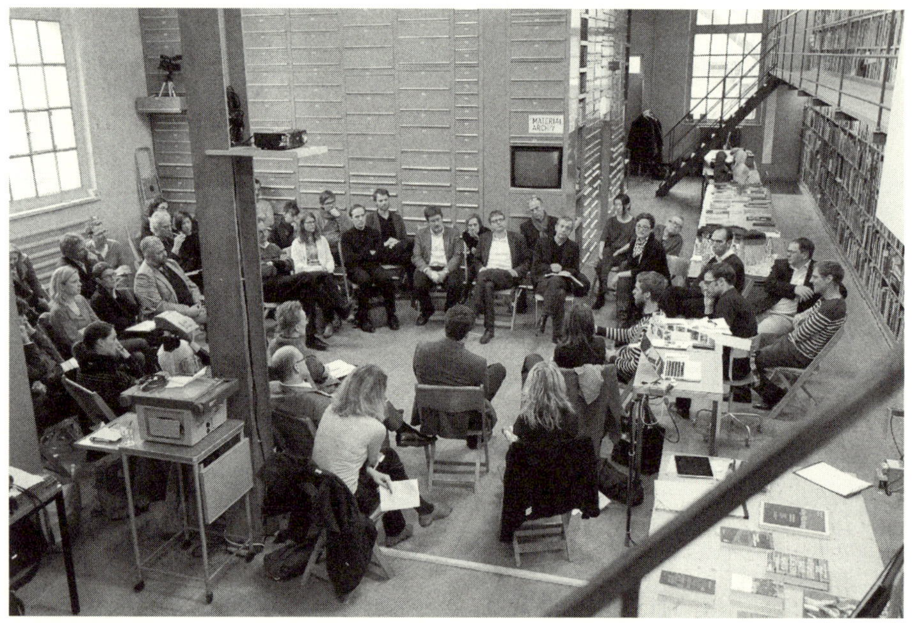

Students doing research in the art library.
The symposium's closing discussion, with all speakers and participants.

16

The Backstory of the Art Library

The following text is based on an unscripted talk given by Felix Lehner during the 2011 *Archive der Zukunft* symposium. Revised to reflect more recent developments at the Sitterwerk, Lehner's contribution describes how dynamic organization principles are playing an increasingly central role and will significantly shape the organization's future. This text also provides an overview of the history of the Sitterwerk, as well as an introduction to Daniel Rohner, an integral figure in the establishment of the art library.

Sitterwerk's art library began as a bequest from the private collection of Daniel Rohner. The library's dynamic organization arose from his highly personal approach to book collecting. Daniel was a lifelong, avid collector of art books in the broadest sense, gathering volumes on design, architecture, photography, and the applied arts. Through thick and thin, he fostered his collection with unwavering intensity.

I met Daniel Rohner after his first exhibition in 1998, when curator Dorothea Strauss mounted an exhibition titled *Wahlverwandschaften* ("Elective Affinities") featuring books from Daniel's collection alongside works from the collection of artist Thomas Kamm, in an exhibition space in Appenzell. Daniel was living in Arbon at the time, in the studio of Peter Kamm, Thomas's brother. A portion of his book collection was there, too.

When I first met him, he had an almost boundless energy—his loud voice and striking appearance filled any space he happened to enter. Later on he fell seriously ill, and although he grew increasingly thin and frail over the nine years that we knew one another, he never lost that unique energy.

As the son of a family of pharmacists in Bern, Daniel came from an upper-middle-class family. He bought his first books in London and Paris, when he was nine years old. He trained as a carpenter, which turned out not to be his true calling, and went on to earn a degree from the Academy of Architecture and Interior Design in Detmold, Germany. While there, he attended countless exhibitions and cultivated relationships with artists and collectors. During this time, he often traveled back and forth between the Ruhr district and Switzerland.

Daniel had a supremely spirited, kind, contradictory, and sometimes difficult personality, and his curious collection of books is a reflection of his strong beliefs. His absolute, uncompromising vision—completely committed to art—was what set him apart and made his collecting possible. He incessantly wrote and transcribed, night after night, list after list. There are boxes upon boxes of lists and auction catalogs. His stacks of paper accumulated and ultimately became an end in and of themselves, keeping him busy. The notes he jotted down didn't necessarily have to be referenced again later, or processed into any other form. The focus wasn't so much about the structure as it was about the instant and intensity of the cataloging work itself. He organized his collection of books, only to then rearrange it. He could completely immerse himself in other worlds, other universes. Each and every surface of any given room held books—all the shelves were filled, and often, even the floor. I admired his book compilations, which every few hours changed into new combinations, but I also marveled at the immense reservoir of associative knowledge he had. If you asked him a question, you needed to have at least two hours on hand if you wanted to hear his full answer. He could end up anywhere, but never went straight there—rather, he meandered with his audience through a world of his own, with himself at the center. You could glean a lot of information from the journey. Universes opened up and just as quickly vanished, and you could only temporarily experience his vast knowledge—volatility was its main characteristic. It was wonderful to get answers along the way, even if the route wasn't the most direct.

We wanted to capture Daniel's information-retrieval process. It was clear to me from the outset that we mustn't lose his highly associative, holistic take on the most far-flung fields of knowledge. I was convinced there had to be a system capable of taking in totally subjective information, while also holding onto otherwise fleeting knowledge. Daniel had no ability to work in a structured way. The "sensory table" that is now a key part of the Sitterwerk library was inspired by Daniel's talent for being blissfully overwhelmed, inspired to such a degree that he came up with fascinating combinations. I thought: "What if the table knew what Daniel set on it, and what if that knowledge could somehow be stored...?" Without Daniel's driven yet unsystematic way of getting distracted while arranging and rearranging the books over and over again, we probably wouldn't have come up with the idea of using dynamic organizing principles, nor would we have had the idea of creating tables and other work surfaces capable of noticing the particular universe of knowledge laid out upon them, and saving that data without much effort. The sensory table's ability to immediately recognize every book means that the feel of each book is taken into account—its size, weight, condition, and even its "scent." On the other hand, of course, what's great about the bookshelf is that, thanks to this principle of dynamic organization, you can come across books for which you were never even looking. So one of our more pragmatic considerations was how to navigate the library's holdings in a more state-of-the-art way. That's what brought us to the idea—back when Daniel was still working in the art library—of dynamic organization and a table that recognizes and stores a list of the books lying on its surface. It interested him only in passing, and just wasn't his main concern. He was certainly a part of the library, and an inspiration for the newly developed classification system, but aside from that, he didn't contribute to its actual conceptual development.

Daniel also felt no real connection with computers, which led us to conclude that the user interface should look differently than the kind normally used in libraries. This means, for example, that we didn't want users to work solely through the keyboard. Computers had to help us in some other way, and let us master various other organizational principles.

In a certain sense, Daniel and I stumbled onto this uncompromising approach—because when the art library was built, everything seemed to go against it. From the very start, the foundry had always included a library, which I managed as best I knew how. My cultural awareness suggested that, outside the workshop itself, part of an institution's importance comes from its library and, by extension, its backstory. The art library's current incarnation was sparked by the creation of the Sitterwerk Foundation in 2006; Hans Jörg Schmid, Daniel Rohner, and I were cofounders. The main goal was to honor sculptor Hans Josephsohn's legacy, and also to give the library greater relevance in relation to the foundry. My friendship with Daniel Rohner gave more considerable weight to the latter. Early on, he made it clear that he liked the idea. His book collections had previously been distributed all across Switzerland, from Geneva to Arbon, including a central warehouse in Bern, where he worked one day a week. These separate holdings were gradually brought together here. We'd have loved for Daniel to work day and night on building this library, but he also had a studio apartment across town, on the edge of the forest, near the Heiligkreuz bus terminal—a sweet set-up with a printshop, its presses still intact.

As the art library developed, we made steady progress. At first, we could only move into part of the building next to the foundry in St.Gallen, but later we moved into the entire space. Lukas Furrer and I were responsible for the architecture, Daniel Rohner for the books. That had been settled at the outset. Although the roles were clearly divided, Daniel nevertheless drew up a lot of plans for the library. He thought having a huge wall of books was a terrible idea. His vision of the library was something else entirely. It would have been a universe in itself—a public library, but not one that could truly come alive.

A retired librarian stepped up to help Daniel develop an overview of the complete holdings. Both were thrilled at the idea, and collaboration began. As a librarian with a classical sense of order, she structured the collection to the best of her ability, working in tandem with Daniel, but his ideas ran completely counter. The incompatibility of their two perspectives became increasingly clear. Within three weeks, their two completely different worlds collided, and Daniel made his will known, so their brief collaboration came to an end.

Financially speaking, in both good and bad times, Daniel made massive acquisitions, which ran him into debt. The Sitterwerk Foundation continued to develop, and eventually Daniel's book collection found its way here. My personal library and that of the foundry were also brought together at Sitterwerk.

The library officially opened in 2006, with an exhibition by Peter Fischli and David Weiss. Daniel complemented their show with a display titled *Bücher, Editionen und Ähnliches* ("Books, Editions, and Such"). Dorothea Strauss gave the introductory talk, and Peter Fischli, David Weiss, Patrick Frey, and many other longtime friends were present, so Daniel was very happy. Fischli and Weiss were working in the foundry at the time, producing a bunch of casts. The exhibition featured preparatory work done on their books, editions, and casts. Another exhibition followed a year later: *Aus dem Off legen: Sechs Verlage für Kunst und ein Sammler* ("Outside the Margins: Six Art Publishers and a Collector"). Seven display cases highlighted the work of six indie publishers—Edizioni Periferia, edition fink, Hans-Peter Feldmann, Barbara Wien, Nieves, and Vexer—arranged throughout the library. Daniel prepared his own table featuring his favorites, gems from his collection of books, which he arranged and described as his "explosives" or his "poison gas chamber." The guest room featured Hans-Peter Feldmann's exquisite work *alle Kleider einer Frau* ("All a Woman's Clothes"), a series of approximately 60 photographs.

Daniel grew sicker and weaker, and was increasingly hospitalized; he spent his last six months in a nursing home next to his apartment. He died just a few months after his second exhibition at Sitterwerk. His last wish was that his ashes be scattered in the Sitter River, and a beautiful celebration was organized to mark the occasion.

The dynamic organizational principles put into practice at Sitterwerk have since been further developed. In addition to the robotic apparatus that runs along the wall of books each day, reading the RFID chips in their spines by means of electromagnetic waves, a newly developed work table is now available, providing yet another research tool. It stems from the "Bibliozine" project, a multi-year initiative developed in collaboration with Christian Kern (InfoMedis), Anthon Astrom and Lukas Zimmer (Astrom/

Zimmer), and Fabian Wegmüller. It explores the dialogue between analog and digital, as well as different ways to visualize the relationships between books and the library's various other materials. The table recognizes and remembers what is on it, and allows users to add notes. It therefore becomes a tool that allows users to compare their own search results with the books and materials currently on display, as well as with the groupings in which these objects were consulted by other library users. As a by-product of this knowledge and cross-referencing, the results of each search can be displayed as a digital document, printed on paper, and bound in the form of a booklet. This facilitates analog research, and can itself be shelved in the form of a so-called Bibliozine, complete with its own RFID tag. The development of the Bibliozine project—but also the library itself— lives through its users. Artists, scientists, and people from many different fields whose curiosity has been piqued continue to come, sometimes spending several days or weeks in the library's guest rooms in order to do their research. The more searches and resulting book compilations are set on the table, the more diverse the Sitterwerk's existing, cross-referenced knowledge base will become, and the more accessible it will be to other users. We look forward to seeing how the Bibliozine will develop as a research tool that is further honed by each successive user.

Felix Lehner
February 2015

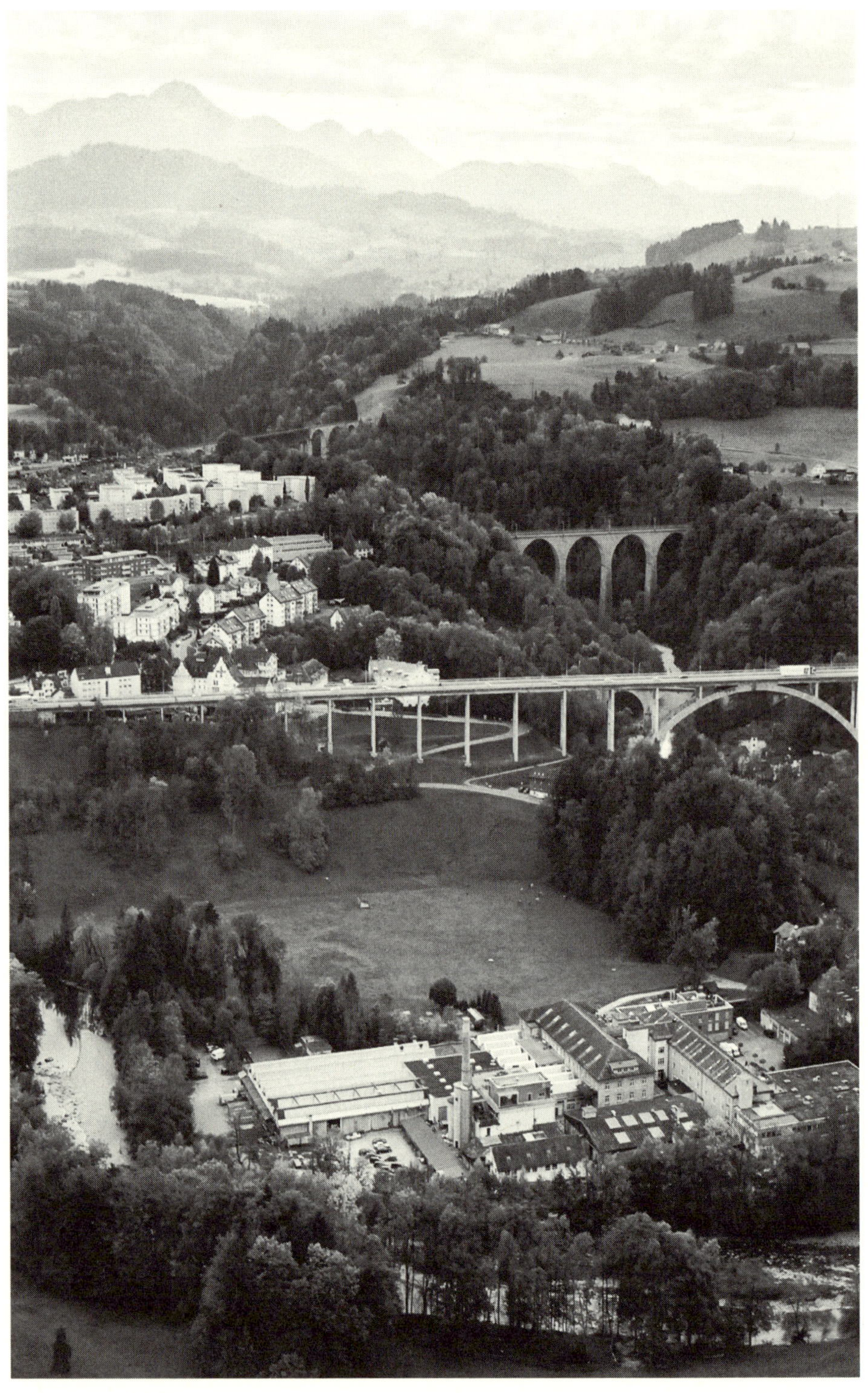

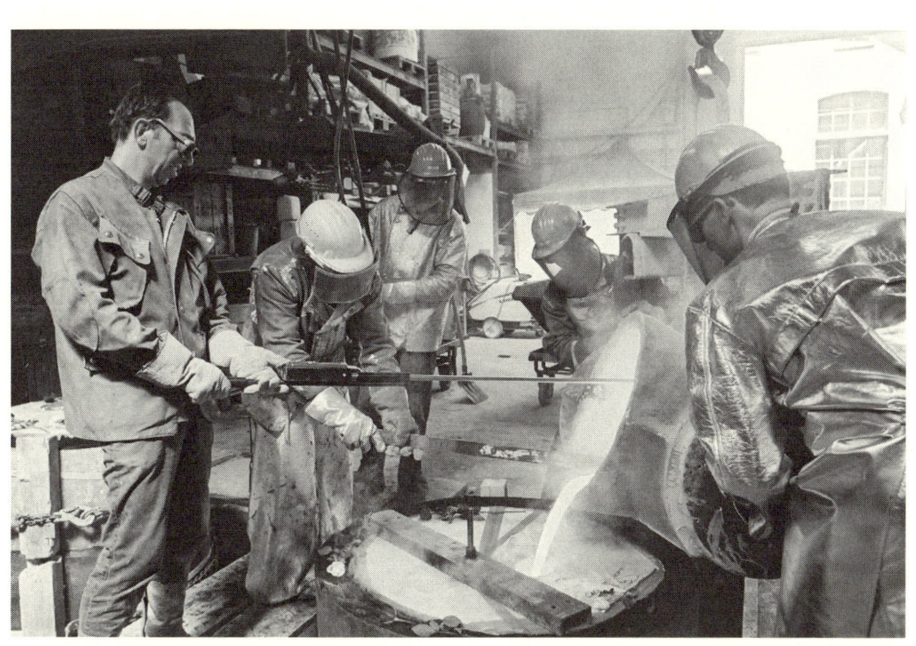

■ The Sitterwerk Foundation includes four divisions—the art library, the material archive, the Kesselhaus Josephsohn, and the studio house—located on the site of the former Sittertal textile dyeworks. ■ The casting process in the neighboring art foundry, where artwork by national and international artists is produced.

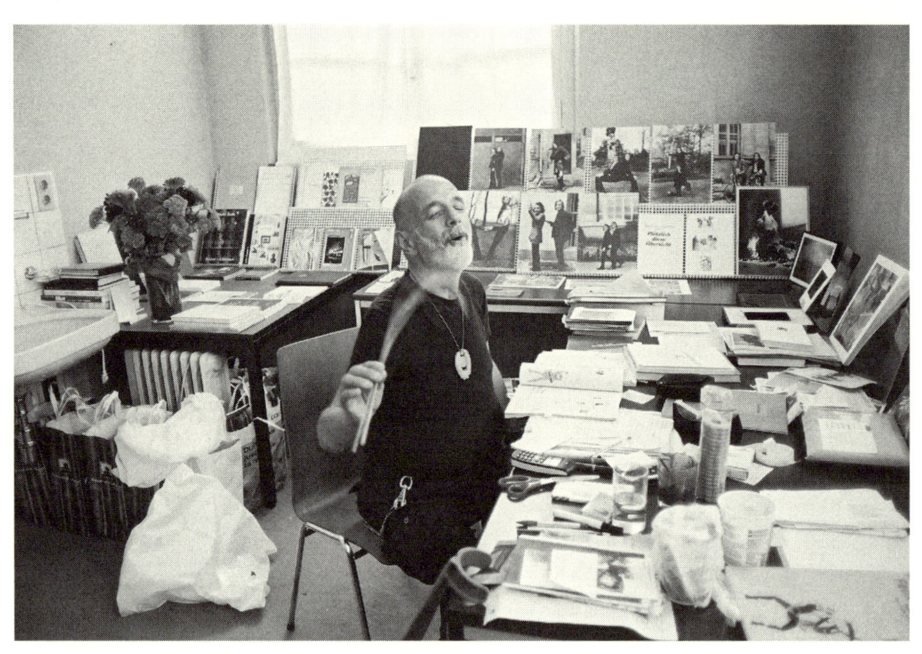

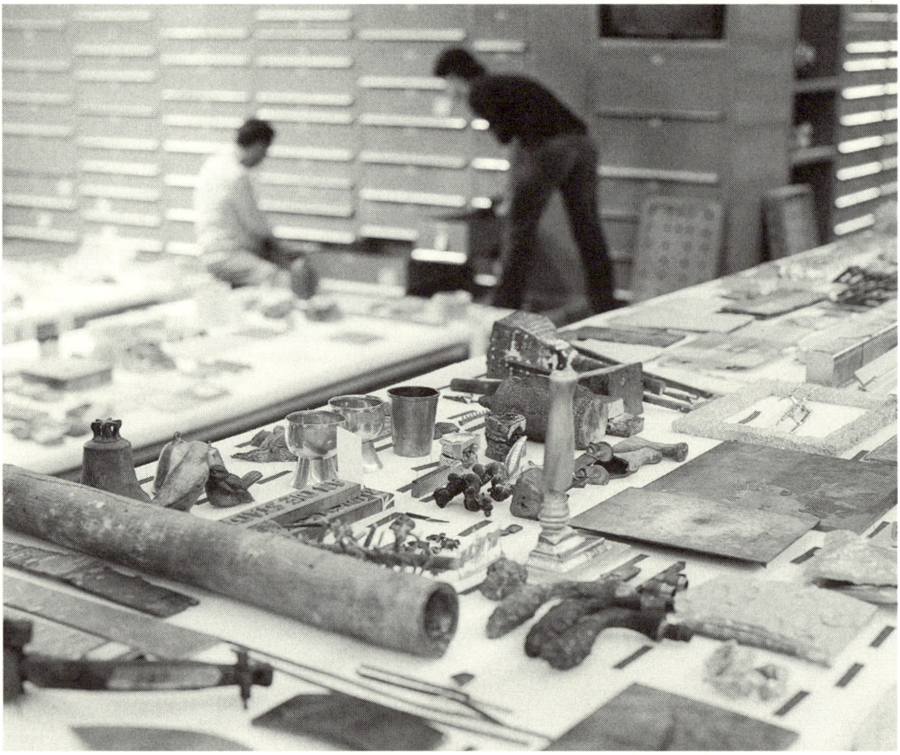

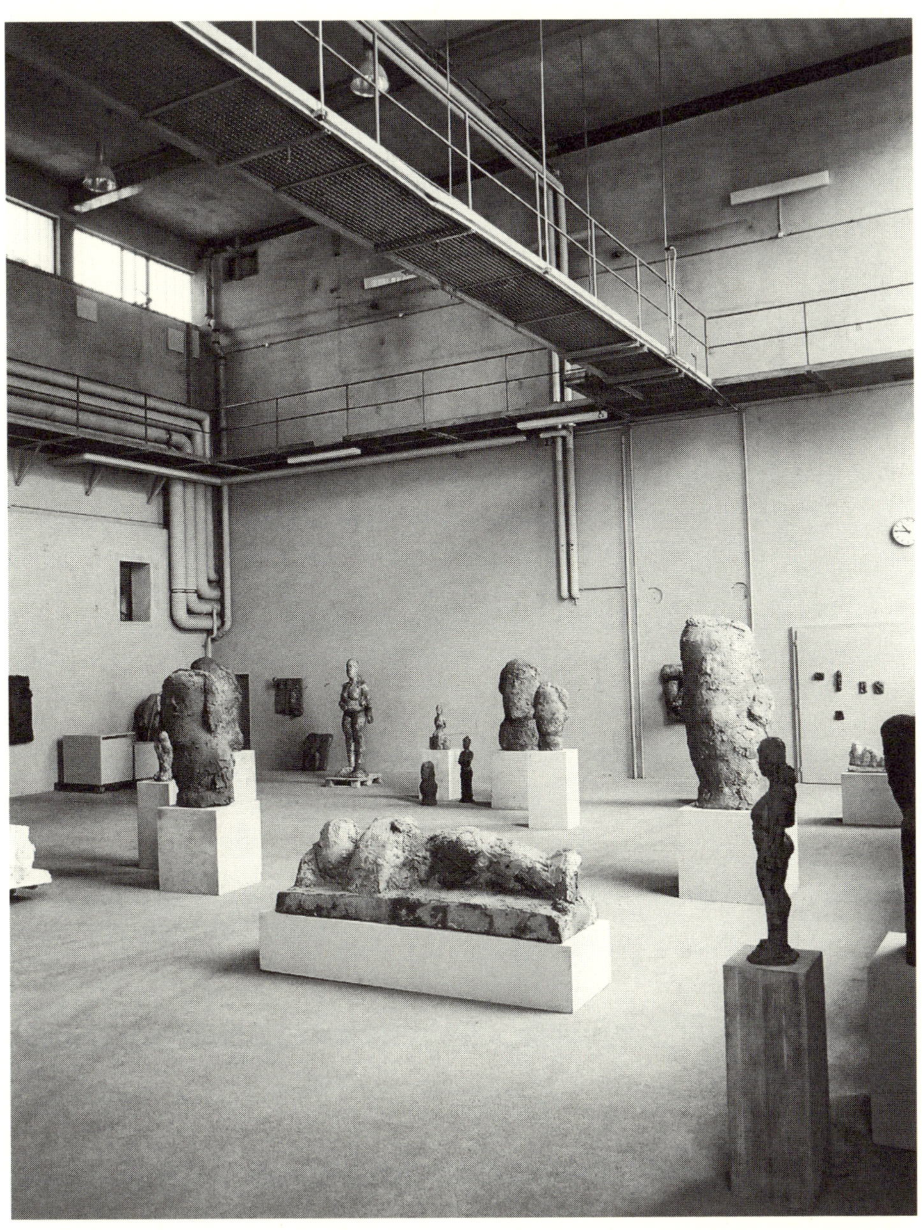

▨ Daniel Rohner (1948–2007), in the art library office. ▨ Cataloging the material archive, summer 2012. ▨ Interior view of the Kesselhaus Josephsohn, an exhibition space where plasters and bronzes by sculptor Hans Josephsohn (1920–2012) are on view ▨ Following spread: A view of the Sitterwerk's art library and material archive.

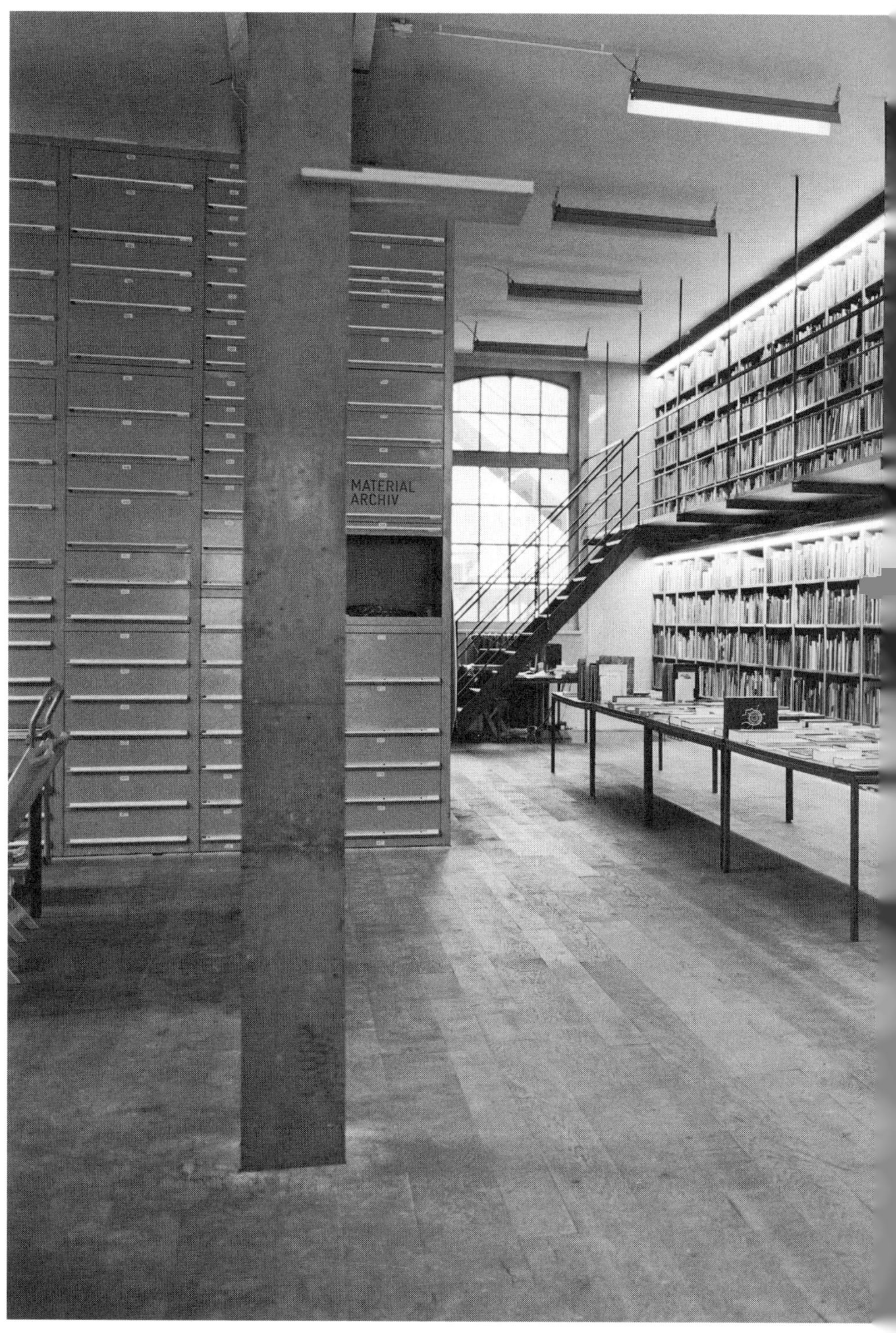
MATERIAL
ARCHIV

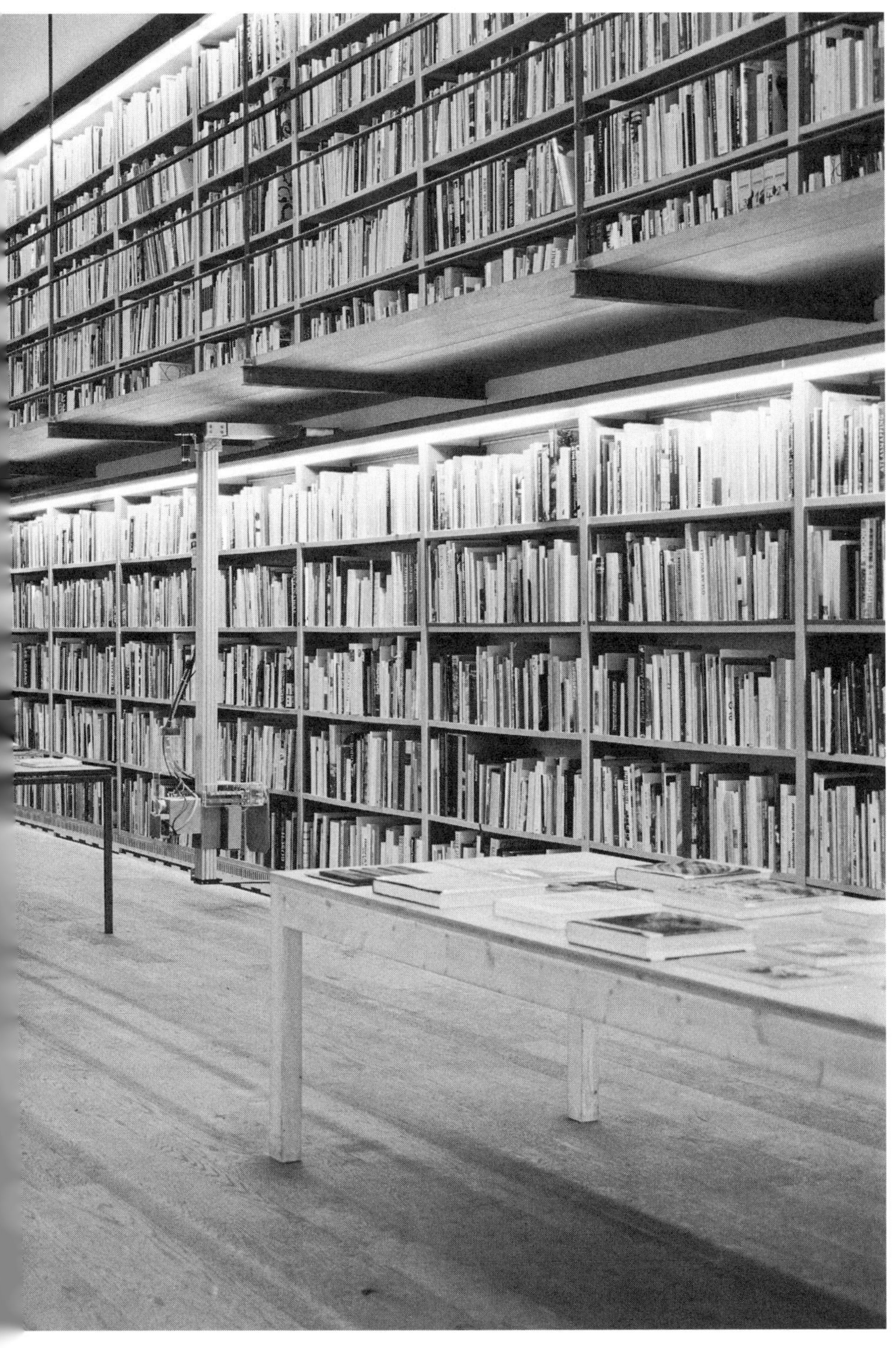

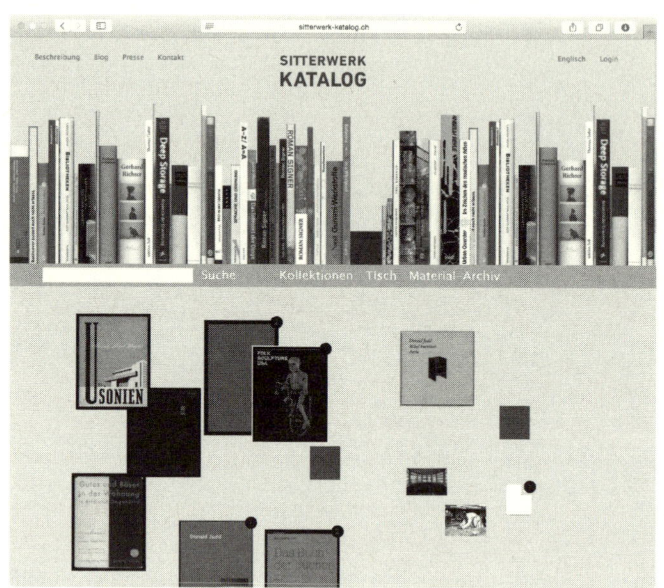

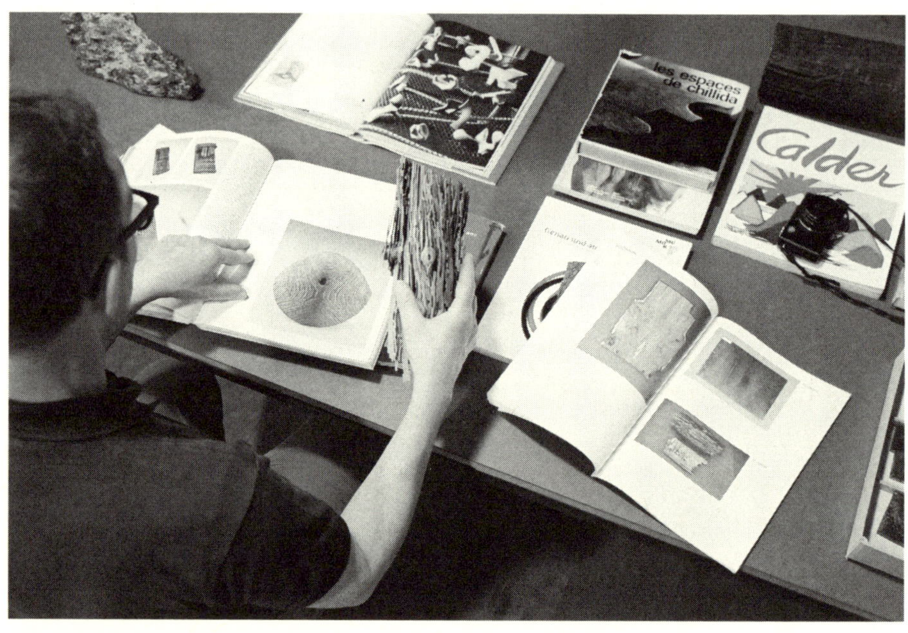

■ The Sitterwerk's digital catalog interface.
■ Doing research in the collections of the art library and material archive. ■ The newly developed workstation for the Bibliozine project: the second version of the RFID-equipped table, 2014.

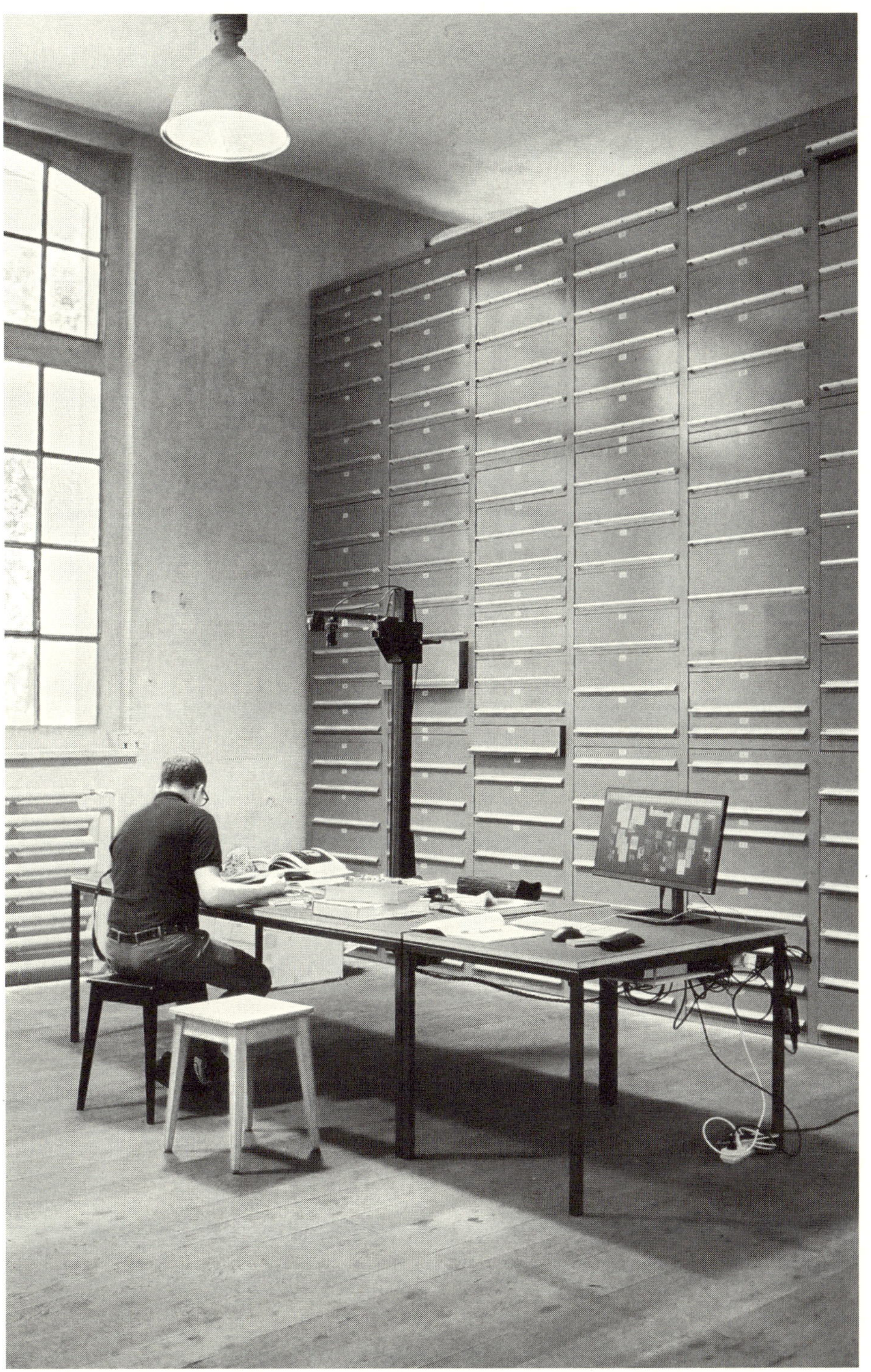

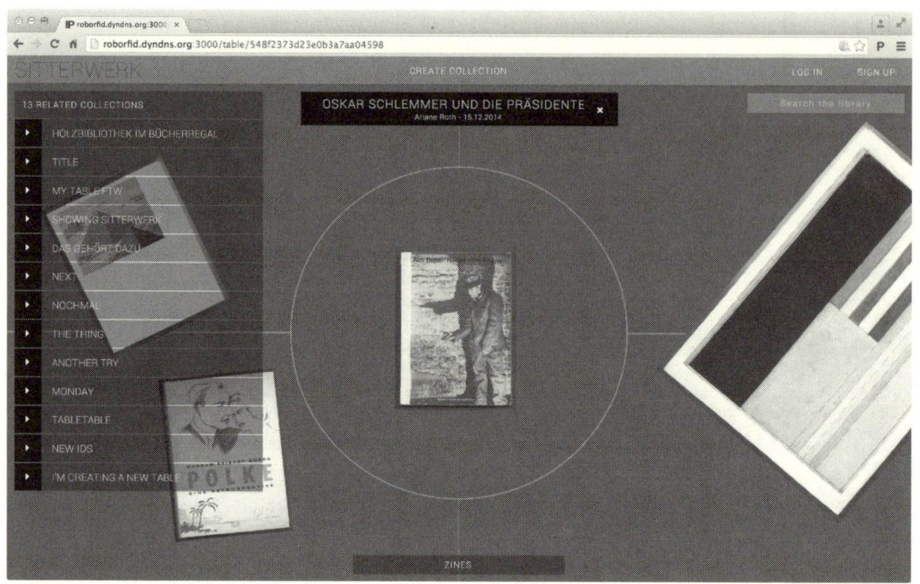

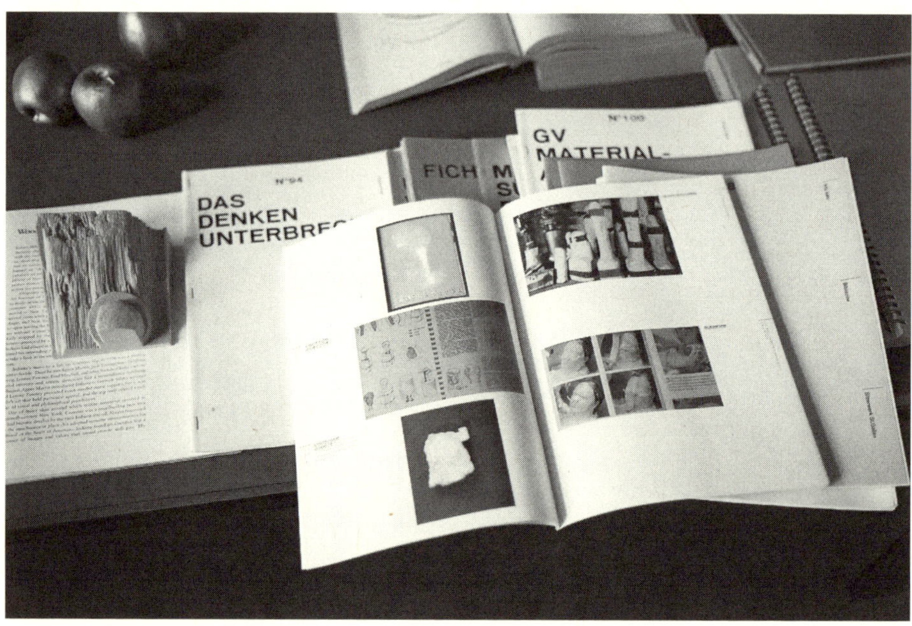

■ The interface of the Bibliozine project. ■ The option of flowing one's research into a "bibliozine" that is then printed out as a pamphlet is just one possibility.

1 CLASSIFICATION SYSTEMS

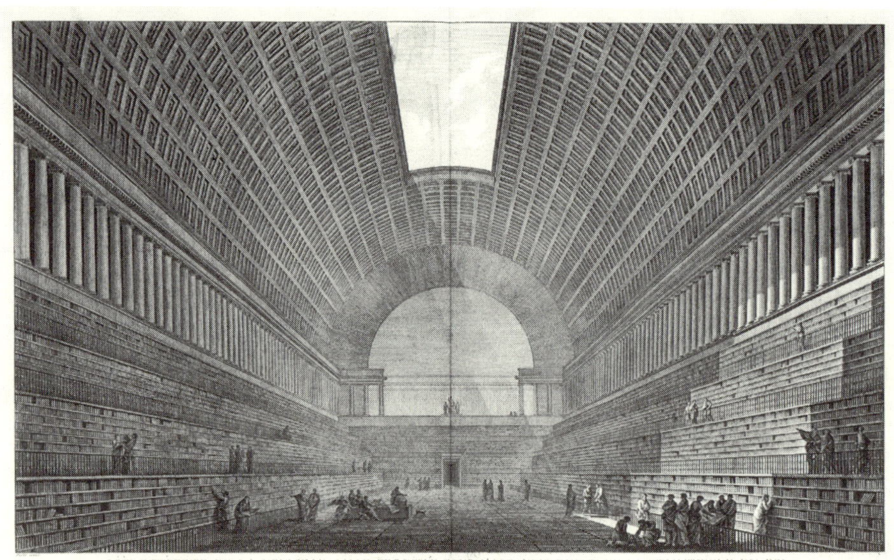

■ *Vue intérieure de la nouvelle salle projetée pour l'agrandissement de la bibliothèque du roi* ("Interior View of the Planned Addition to the King's Library"), Étienne-Louis Boullée, 1785.

Introduction

"Order is what turns a mere collection of books into a library." The ideal coda to this oft-cited phrase might well be: because libraries are not an end in themselves, but are closely linked to their users, their order must generally be clear and understandable—at least for their particular public.

In recent years, the field of information science has dealt primarily with issues of how searches can be conducted using huge digital storage devices. Relational databases and hypertext have opened up new search options. As a whole, however, the sheer quantity of information is vast, and most of it remains hidden from view. It doesn't seem to have any real classification system, so we ultimately end up searching amid the cloudy waters of a murky sea.

Even in ancient times, and again in the Renaissance, our ancestors sought to organize all extant knowledge. The Enlightenment ushered in a more scientific approach, as thinkers attempted to develop all-encompassing organization and classification systems. One of the earliest and most well-known examples is Jean Baptiste le Rond d'Alembert's "tree of knowledge."

These systems were then used to organize libraries. By the eighteenth century, reference libraries became fully established, complete with splendid baroque architecture. The Imperial Library in Vienna is just one example—princes, kings, and emperors built baroque libraries in order to present their knowledge of the world as accurately as possible, and in the most dignified setting. In this world order, each subject and every book had its proper place. In order to find a given book, you had to know its place in this linear formation, even if it was in the very last row. In 1785, Étienne-Louis Boullée strove to preserve this organizational/architectural principle in his design for a gigantic library, but it was already too late. The rapidly increasing volume of knowledge made available by print could no longer be handily organized and laid out in a traditional space.

In the nineteenth century, books began to disappear into closed stacks. The only books that remained in reading rooms were reference volumes and book directories in the form of catalogs. One and the same book could now be listed on several catalog cards—knowledge's new deputies—and organized into different classification systems. This, however, meant that the book was reduced to a call number, which became the only detail readily accessible to library users. In the latter half of the twentieth century, many libraries brought their books back from the stacks and placed them on open shelves. All the while, of course, they maintained the catalogs, so users now had direct access to both the book's deputy (the card catalog), as well as the original itself. And still the library strove to maintain a concrete order across shelves, stacks, and catalogs.

Is such an approach even desirable today? Can we still use linear, analytical, rigidly organized classification systems to feasibly promote interdisciplinary thinking and research? In addition to epistemological interests, might there be epistemological classification systems as well? Or do such outdated systems simply hinder innovation? Why is the researcher's own knowledge so rarely recognized as an asset in and of itself—one worth integrating into the system? Can associative systems lead us to new knowledge, or merely confuse us? These are just a few of the many questions that automatically arise when dealing with classification systems. The following three contributions explore these and many other questions in more detail.

Gerhard Matter

Organizing Knowledge

Coping with Information Overload

When the sum total of knowledge is greater than what can be stored in one's head, or when it becomes necessary to share knowledge between people (especially across generations), the problem of retrieval becomes an issue (from the French *retrouver*, "to find again," which must be distinguished from *discovery*).

It isn't the sheer quantity—now measured in terabytes—of stored knowledge that troubles us today; previous generations also fought a similarly perceived flood of information. Johann Heinrich Zedler's *Grosse vollständige Universal-Lexicon aller Wissenschafften und Künste* ("Great Complete Encyclopedia of All Sciences and Arts"), published between 1732 and 1754, runs to 63,000 pages and encompasses approximately 284,000 entries, issued in 64 volumes.

Retrieval Techniques

Depending on the medium, there are various techniques:
  · in an oral culture, mnemonics such as "My Very Eager Mother
    Just Served Us Nothing = Mercury, Venus, Earth, Mars,
    Jupiter, Saturn, Uranus, Neptune"
  · in a written culture, alphabetized lists; in an IT culture, full-text
    search (possibly combined with Boolean word search)

All such techniques have their drawbacks: full-text search, for example, doesn't factor in lemmatization or homonym detection; searching for *mouse* will not bring up *mice*, but it will bring up both the rodent and the computer pointing device.

There are several basic techniques for retrieving specific bits of knowledge:
  · industrious, unthinking slaves (professor to assistant: "Give this
    book a quick read and see if you find anything on x," a task
    now relegated to robots)
  · complexity reduction, i.e., bits of information are linked to others,
    and exist within a structure familiar to the researcher and/or easy
    to remember; this includes identifying lemmata and key words
  · maintaining a specific order

Organization and Classification

In the entry on encyclopedias in his *Encyclopédie, ou Dictionnaire raisonné des sciences, des arts et des métiers*, Diderot writes:[1] "[T]he possible systems of human knowledge are as numerous as those points of view. The only one from which arbitrariness is excluded…is the system which has existed from all eternity in the will of God."

Such systems depend on one's point of view and are, therefore, culturally specific. In order to understand the relativity of one's own position, one can consider foreign cultures, or travel back into the past as it was experienced by our ancestors. Here, too, there are some general techniques suited to everyone:

- We humans have a good grasp on spatial orientation. This can be put to use—as it is, for instance, on most computer desktops, which feature a graphical user interface: it's easy for us to see (and remember) whether we stored the icon of a file on the top left, etc.
- We can memorize stories well. Narrative links have been used in medieval encyclopedias and many other cognitive devices.

Throughout history, many classification systems have been devised to meet the needs of whoever might be doing the research (be it children, farmers, priests, party animals, et al.).

Knowledge

What is knowledge? This one word paves the way for a wide variety of things. There are many different types of knowledge, different types of logic, different degrees of certainty, different kinds of interconnection, etc.

Knowledge functions as a network. In order to be called up or stored, it must be broken up into its constituent elements. By jotting bits of information on cards and storing them in catalogs, a book's well-built knowledge structure is destroyed. The upshot is that the user can then recombine those elements into new configurations.[2]

With hyperlinks (which appeared in Diderot's encyclopedia as *renvois*, and again in Ted Nelson's *Project Xanadu*, from 1960) makeshift elements are reunited. The result is a semantic network, but it's made by whoever writes the encyclopedia (usually an editorial team), and so the user remains dependent. Such links are best for calling up insight within already known contexts, so the user can move farther down the same path, but rarely result in any real breakthrough.

Knowledge exists only within the context of practical, applicable life experience. For example: botany books don't usually have an entry for *weed*, but gardeners know quite well what they have to yank up by the roots. Unclean animals usually aren't listed in zoology books, but observant Jews know full well that they can only eat the meat of ruminants with cloven hooves (Leviticus 11:3–8). Because bits of knowledge are so multifaceted, they can also pop up in different places within the same classification system. (A coin can be categorized according to economic value, or as a numismatic element classified by size; it makes little difference.)

Access to Knowledge

In a traditional encyclopedia or conventional library catalog (as cards in drawers), these bits of knowledge are called up with tags, lemmata, key words, etc., and users grab onto these pointers—if they even know the lemmata and how they work!

- This results in an interface problem: the encyclopedia author or librarian must anticipate the possible search queries users are apt to look up, and, vice versa, users must know the keywords' synonyms or the system itself.
- Until recently, knowledge was mono-directional: the encyclopedia or library "made knowledge available," i.e., experts provided information, and users received it. The natural question: might the knowledge of the user somehow be put to use?

One perennial problem is the quality of the search technique: users want to find all possible results, but only the relevant ones—they don't want to miss anything relevant, but don't want to draw any blanks. But who determines what's relevant?

Wild Goose Chases

Indexing or applying a keyword to any element or piece of knowledge involves reading into it, such that other interpretations could potentially be arrived at, and something is invariably excluded from this classification as well. Classification systems are "knowledge directing" (Jürgen Habermas), but this also applies in an authoritarian sense. For example, Krünitz's encyclopedia has no entry for "child labor," but of course, it is mentioned everywhere, under other names: the entry on "sewing needles," for one, describes how they're made and mentions that children [presumably because of their tiny fingers] carry out many parts of the process.[3]

Add to that the recent advent of more "personalized" search functions, which try to help but often turn out to be treacherous, excluding the often fertile stroke of serendipity and coincidence.[4] As a result, a library staff's assistance, encyclopedias' editorial teams, and robotic Internet search engines often inadvertently lead researchers astray.

Order is not always very fruitful.[5] Innovations (entailing real discovery, not mere retrieval) are often inspired by fuzzy searches and serendipity.

The words of Louis Pasteur (1822–95) come to mind: "Where observation is concerned, chance favors only the prepared mind."[6] In order to empower researchers to resist the seduction of overly narrow classifications, hits should be sought across multiple subcategories. For example, "travel" should be considered as it relates to geography, social engineering, a means of transport, etc. You never know—maybe the natives of Fiji categorize travel and travel agencies under "mythology." Similarly, books in Sitterwerk's library are categorized according to how they pertain to various, often vastly different contexts.

The Researcher's Knowledge

The idea that you can simply "tap into" any given source of knowledge (sages, encyclopedias, libraries) is misleading. It doesn't take into account that fact that, consciously or unconsciously, the person doing the search brings certain types of knowledge along with them.

Certain types of prior knowledge can help filter one's viewpoint or focus the field of inquiry:
  · the language in which keywords are written and in
    which they will be searched
  · textbook knowledge
  · knowledge of one's own life experience
  · prejudices / opinions / *idées fixes*

Each user also brings certain meta-skills to their search:
  · that most textbooks have useful indexes
  · that homonyms must be taken into account, or further
    searches must be done using synonyms
  · that a library or other catalog can suggest additional
    keywords to search under, etc.

Each search process is conditioned by contextual factors:
  · need
  · interest
  · expectation

It's interesting to look at the discussion pages of Wikipedia to see how users try to find a consensus on what can be considered reliable knowledge. Here, for the first time, the negotiations involved in defining what constitutes knowledge are visible to everyone; this process used to take place in esoteric laboratories, university seminars, and encyclopedias' editorial departments. As a result, we get the distinct impression that knowledge is constantly changing. In the past, when new editions came out every thirty years or so, that wasn't at all the case.

Queries

Who is looking for what—which questions are being asked, and what search strategies do users employ as they wind their way through a dictionary or library? (Picture this: you're a Swiss librarian and someone comes up to the desk and says, in dialect, "Got anything on Muslim weddings?"). Is there such a thing as the hermeneutics of querying?

What do "knowledge gaps" actually look like (in the logical, hermeneutic sense)? For starters, we might distinguish between:
  - narrow queries—for instance, "What are Kalmyks?"
    (Wh-questions)
  - follow-up queries—for instance, "How is Impressionism
    defined in music?"
  - open queries, which aim to discover something new

How can you find out what you don't yet know? Can encyclopedias/libraries encourage users to ask more complex questions? Is that their job, or should it be taught in the classroom instead? One of Brecht's characters comes to mind: "'I have noticed,' said Mr. K., 'that we put many people off our teaching because we have an answer to everything. Could we not, in the interests of propaganda, draw up a list of the questions that appear to us completely unsolved?'"[7]

Social Tagging

The technical foundations for the phenomena outlined in *The Wisdom of Crowds*[8]—*folksonomy* (a portmanteau of *folk* and *taxonomy*, coined in 2003) and "social tagging"—were made possible by the Internet. Users are no longer merely recipients of information, they can now provide their own information. This allows multiple users to collaboratively (and often unchecked by any authority) provide a piece of information using catchwords. These aren't keywords in the strict sense of the term, because they don't necessarily adhere to any established vocabulary—there's no underlying thesaurus. The debate over the advantages and disadvantages of this approach is ongoing:[9]
  - Skeptics of authority and supposed expertise are pleased that
    things are now more democratic.
  - This approach allows one and the same bit of knowledge to
    be classified differently, depending on perspective, which helps
    combat narrow-mindedness and unlocks new insights.
  - The user's knowledge is involved. But are a bunch of anony-
    mous users actually any smarter than a library pro?
  - Exactly who is collaborating here? Bots, amateurs, weirdos, ex-
    perts—or even spammers, crazies, and haters? Shouldn't a

rating system be introduced, depending on the degree of the contri-
butors' professionalism?

· This approach entails various problems: case sensitivity, semantic
disambiguation, tags' hierarchy, etc.

· Should formatting guidelines to the tagging community be drawn up?

· Should "wildcard" tags be dealt with in a certain way? Or wouldn't
that be a betrayal of the ideas underlying Web 2.0?

Supposed Completeness

Systematic, orderly classifications are not just a way of finding things, they
also express pride: knowledge—we've got you, you're all ours!

· A taxonomy begins with the trunk of the tree, on which all bran-
ches, twigs, and fruits depend.

· Even the "all-phabet" can become a stranglehold of sorts: there's
no bit of knowledge that can escape, everything can be fit into
the all-encompassing space between the alpha and the omega.

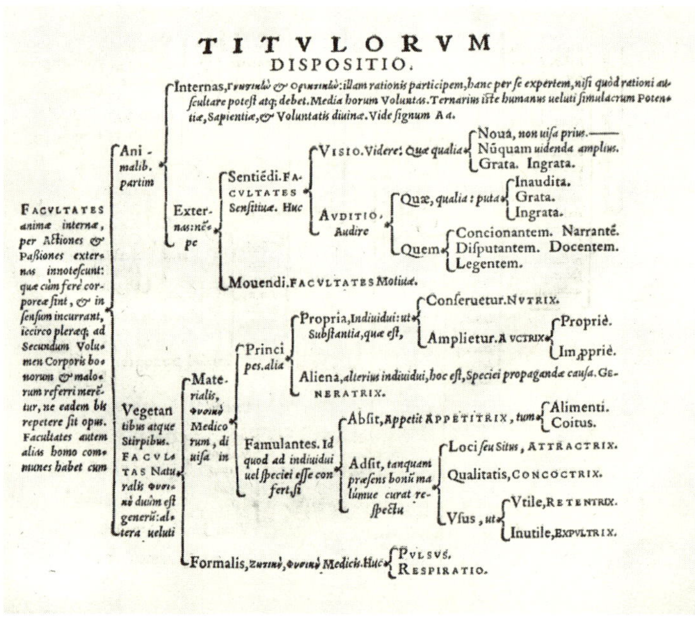

Theodor Zwinger, *Theatrum Humanae Vitae
Theodoris Zvingeri Bas., Tertiatione Nouem Volumi-
nibus locupletatum, interpolatum, renouatum. cum
tergemino Elencho, Methodi scilicet, Titulorum &
Exemplorum. Basileae: per Evsebium Episcopivm*
(Basel, 1586–87).

Appendix:

A Selection of Organizing Principles Used in Early Encyclopedias

A word to history haters who might protest that medieval classification systems are old hat, and wonder what could they possibly be worth today: When it comes to steering clear of delusion, casting off our blinders, and battling hegemonic monocultures—these are all things we want, right?—we need to broaden our horizons. This can easily be done by letting in foreign ideas ("letting in" is the opposite of "colonizing"—to put it in commercial terms: what do we import and what do we export, and how much?). Getting to know the unfamiliar is a way to avoid getting trapped within one set point of view. The unfamiliar might be defined geographically (Eastern vs. Western culture) or temporally (the medieval era vs. the present day). In-depth investigations can and often should lead to a degree of discomfort: "Hmm, so it could be seen that way, too, and the causes are *x* and the results are *y*." Such exploration exposes the fact that our views might not be truly objective, but are instead culturally and historically relative.

The following sections give a few examples. For each classification system/organizing principle (defined by what structure connects these bits of knowledge/information) we briefly outline: (A) the target user and context (who benefits, and what they need to know in order to navigate it); and (B) the cost-benefit analysis (what's being simplified, and the difficulties and solutions it entails). Such considerations apply not only to remote historical events, but also to current developments.

FROM THE GENERAL TO THE SPECIFIC—TAXONOMIC ORDER

Examples: Theodor Zwinger, 1533–88; Johann Heinrich Alsted, 1588–1638; the Dewey Decimal System.

> The search begins with the most general: everything that exists. That can be further divided into physical and non-physical. The physical can be further divided into living and dead. The living can be further divided into animate and inanimate. The animate can be further divided into mortal and immortal. The mortal—in this case, animals—can be further divided into quadrupeds, birds, fish, insects, etc.

(A) User must know the system, but can then conduct relatively open searches.

(B) Things that belong together are grouped accordingly, and the system works independent of language; potentially problematic when one element is found in several subdivisions. The branching structure, from the most general down to the finest nuance, can be represented as a tree easily depicted typographically using brackets.

Example: Thomas Cantimpratensis, † ca. 1270, *Liber de natura rerum*; Konrad von Megenberg, 1309–74, *Buch von der Natur*.

Bits of information are arranged in descending order, from the noblest to the most base—from the human soul down to lowly lead. (The test question used to assess the dignity of each mortal element: Have you ever killed a bunny rabbit, a fish, an insect? The answer determines its place in the noble/base hierarchy.)

On man & hys generel natur
brain, hair, sleep, cheekes, cheste, heart, bile, kidneys, sygns of whether a wifman is wyth childe, of the countenance of man, of feet, of constitution, of dreams, &c.
On heven and the seven planetes
On anymals
the first to roam earth
on foweles
on sea creatures
on fisches
on snaykes
on wurms (also spyders, silkworms, antes, flyes, maggots)
On bereys, on fyne-taysting bereys
On herbes
wurmwud, garlick, wundwort, saffran, millet, minth, watercresse, shuger, &c.
On precious gemes
On smything [= metals]: gold, silver, qwicksilver, … zynck, led.

(A) This system heavily depends on cultural cues.
(B) Less effective for finding specific help; more effective as a demonstration of the general order of the entire cosmos.

AS CURRICULUM OR SYLLABUS

Example: Gregor Reisch c.1470–1525, *Margarita Philosophica*, 1503.

In medieval schools students first learned Latin, were then trained in the trivium and quadrivium, and finally completed specialized study in either philosophy, medicine, law, or theology. Current school curricula follow the same general structure (note the architectural metaphor): first basic skills are taught (the foundations); then students step upward (in grades or levels), until they enter higher education.

(A) Intended for teachers and students; no special knowledge required.
(B) Natural growth of knowledge. Students who fail the final exam repeat
that period of study.

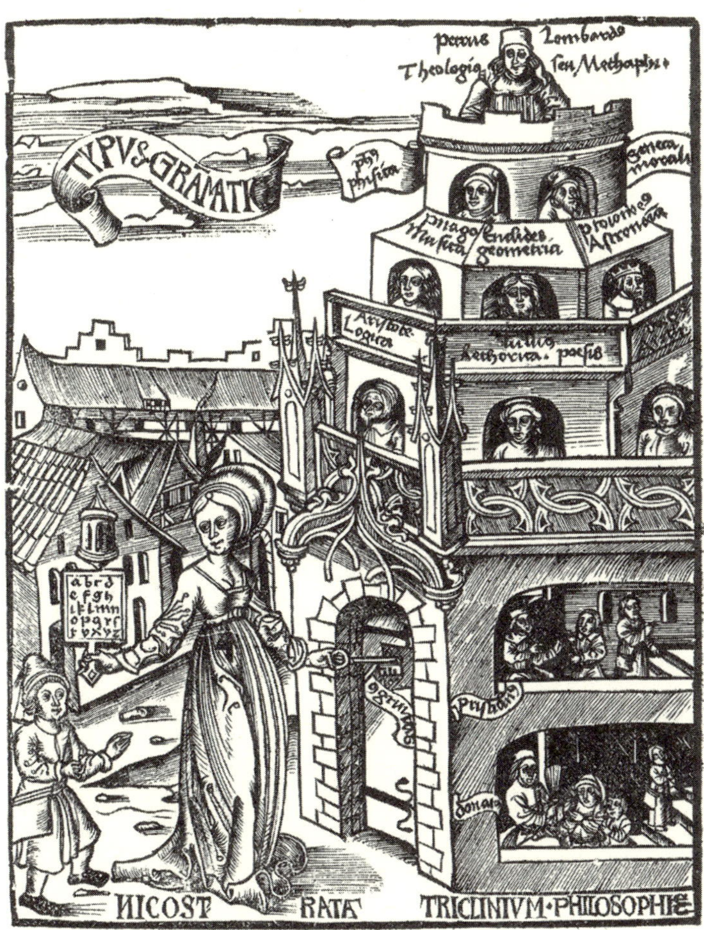

Gregor Reisch, *Aepitoma omnis phylosophiae,
alias Margarita Phylosophica tractans de omni ge-
nere scibili* (Freiburg, 1503).

43

ACCORDING TO THE SIX DAYS OF CREATION

Example: Saint Ambrose, c. 340–97, *Hexameron*.

Day of creation according to Genesis 1:1–31 (six days of creation)...	...gives occasion to discuss:
1st day: heaven and empty earth; light, and thus day and night are created.	god as creator; evil; time
2nd day: the firmament is created to divide the water below the earth from the water above the earth.	separation of the spheres; the parts of the ocean, its use
3rd day: land and sea are separated; plants are created.	botany; agriculture; poison plants and remedies; wine; fruit cultivation; grafting
4th day: stars, sun, and moon are brought to the sky.	use of sunlight; polemic against astrology; annual cycles; the moon, which causes ebb and flow
5th day: fish and fowl are created.	zoology I; water as a life-giving element; food chain; "intelligence" of fish; salt; coral; navigation; birds and their intelligent behavior; beehives
6th day: land animals and, finally, people are created.	zoology II; animals' anatomy, instincts, and reproduction; anthropology; beauty of the human body; the soul

(A) Jews/Christians who know the first 31 verses of the Bible will be able to find their way around.

(B) Applies to everything, since it's founded on theonomy; theologically all-encompassing, but not detailed enough for modern science.

ACCORDING TO THE CATECHISM

Example: Antoine d'Averoult, S. J., *Les fleurs des exemples*, 1603.

This work contains exemplary stories, legends, and other devotional materials for preachers, organized thematically: creed, the ten commandments, the seven sacraments, the seven cardinal virtues and the seven deadly sins, the works of mercy, the four last things.

(A) Priests, who know the categories by heart.

(B) Ensures rapid answers to all kinds of religious questions (just think of the Saturday-night plight preachers feel as they prepare material on a specific topic for their Sunday service).

We all know this one from dictionaries. This system is—aside from its use in dictionaries—not that old. Hübner's 1704 *Conversationslexicon* was the first German encyclopedia organized alphabetically.

(A) Laypeople; most can recite the ABCs by heart.
(B) Relevant lemma/word roots must be known/guessed; interconnections are lost; encyclopedias cannot easily be translated into another language without significant reorganization.

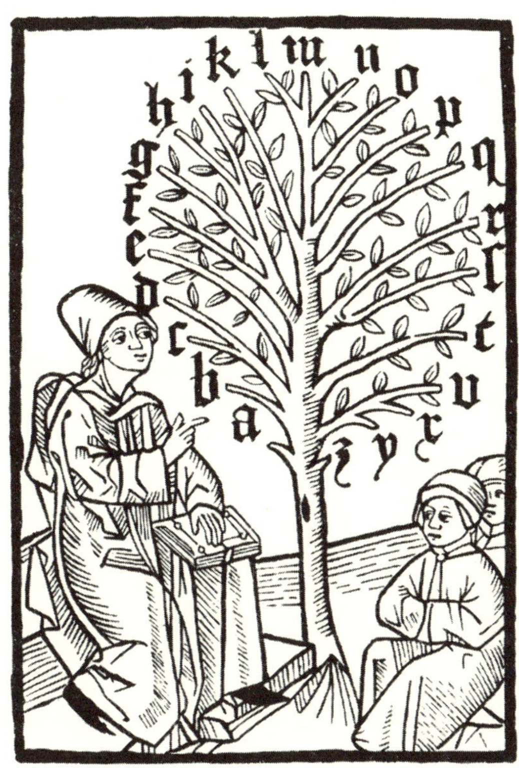

■ *Ein heylsame lere vnd predig des Würdigen Hochgelehrten docters Doctor Johansen Geiler von Keysersberg* (Ulm: J. Zainer, 1490). Reprinted in: *Emil Reicke, Magister und Scholaren. Illustrierte Geschichte des Schulwesens* (Leipzig: Diderichs, 1901), p. 58.

LVII.

Convivium.   **Die Mahlzeit.**

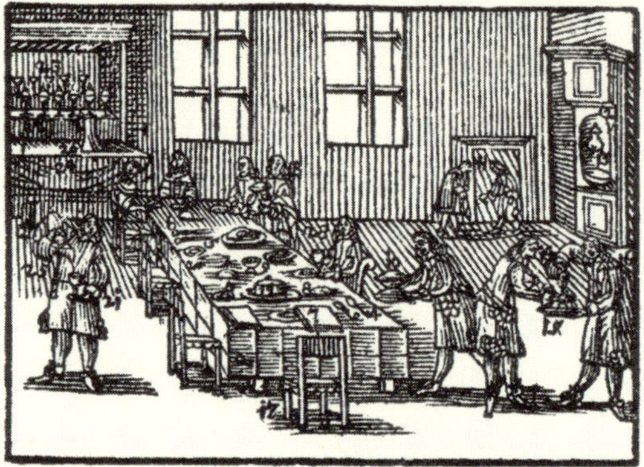

Cum apparatur	Wann angestellt wird
Convivium,	eine Mahlzeit/
Mensa sternitur	wird der Tisch (Tafel)
Tapetibus 1	gedeckt mit Teppichen 1
& *Mappâ*, 2	und dem Tischtuch 2
à *Triclinariis*,	von den Tafeldeckern/
qui prætereà apponunt	welche überdas auflegen
Discos. (Orbes) 3	die Teller/ 3
Cochlearia, 4	Löffeln/ 4
Cultros, 5	Messer 5
cum *Fuscinulis*, 6	und Gabeln / 6
Mappulas, 7	Tellertüchlein/ 7
Panem 8	Brod 8

cum

■ Johann Amos Comenius, *Orbis Sensualium Pictus […] Die sichtbare Welt / Das ist Aller vornemsten Welt-Dinge und Lebens-Verrichtungen Vorbildung und Benahmung* (Nürnberg: Endter, 1658; Reprint: *Die bibliophilen Taschenbücher* 30 [Dortmund: Harenberg, 1978]).

Example: Johann Amos Comenius, 1592–1670, *Orbis sensualium pictus*, and many later picture dictionaries, including *Bilder-Duden*.

(A) Anyone (including specialists; for example, to see all components of a car engine).
(B) Context and interrelationships are maintained. The index helps the user find an individual bit of information within a larger cluster.

Paul Michel

Encyclopedias:

- Konrad von Megenberg (1309–74), *Buch der Natur*, ed. Franz Pfeiffer. Stuttgart: Aue-Verlag, 1861.
- Ambrosius Mediolanensis (340–97), *Hexaemeron*, in *Patrologia Latina* (tomus 14, col. 123–274). Paris, 1845.
- Antoine d'Averoult S. J., *Les Fleurs des exemples ou Catechisme historial*, (*Contenant plusieurs Miracles & excellens discours, tirez tant de l'Escriture Saincte que des Saincts Peres, & anciens docteurs des l'eglise. Livre tres vtile pour les Curez, Predictateurs, & à tous vrays amateurs de la doctrine Chrestienne. Suyvant les chapitres, & matieres due Catechisme du concile de trente*). Paris, 1603.

1 "Le nombre des systèmes possibles de la connoissance humaine est aussi grand que celui des points de vue. Le seul, d'où l'arbitraire seroit exclu, c'est le système qui existait de toute éternité dans la volonté de Dieu." Denis Diderot, "Encyclopedia," trans. Philip Stewart (Ann Arbor: University of Michigan Library, 2002). Originally published as "Encyclopédie," *Encyclopédie ou Dictionnaire raisonné des sciences, des arts et des métiers*, 5:635–648A (Paris, 1755). 2 Cf. Karl W. Bührer or Vannevar Bush. 3 Johann Georg Krünitz (founding ed.), *Oekonomischtechnologische Encyklopädie, oder allgemeines System der Staats Stadt Haus und Land Wirthschaft und der Kunstgeschichte* 101 [1806], p. 4. 4 Cf. the excellent article by Miriam Meckel (*Neue Zürcher Zeitung*, 20 September 2011, p. 58).

5 "Ich erkenne die ungeheuren Vorteile der Schlamperei." ("I recognize the tremendous benefits of sloppiness.") Bertolt Brecht, *Flüchtlingsgespräche*. 6 "Dans les champs de l'observation le hazard ne favorise que les espirits préparés." Louis Pasteur. [From a lecture given at the University of Lille, 7 December 1854—Trans.] 7 Bertolt Brecht, *Stories of Mr. Keuner*, trans. Martin Chalmers (San Francisco: City Lights, 2001): p. 18. 8 James Surowiecki, *The Wisdom of Crowds* (New York: Doubleday, 2004). 9 Cf. Isabella Peters and Katrin Weller, "Tag gardening for folksonomy enrichment and maintenance," *Webology* 5(3), 2008, Article 58.

Library Organization Systems

Although the misguided idea that libraries are simply large storerooms for books is complicated by the many other functions and tasks these institutions fulfill, here I shall nevertheless focus on their extensive holdings and the systems by which they're stored in both shelves and stacks. The collection and preservation of media is one of the library's most important tasks, so the organization of their holdings is a central and indispensable subject. How these holdings are sorted depends on many factors: format/size, library type, available space, and institutional philosophy. To a certain extent, the history of the institution itself can be inferred from a library's chosen system and its design, because each era has created its own organizing principles for its libraries. I shall give a brief chronological outline and overview—regrettably quite condensed—of the broad range of classification systems in libraries.

Inventory/Location/Catalogs

Medieval libraries had readily manageable holdings, literally speaking—most items were within arm's reach. The "natural form"[1] by which to organize them was as an open-access library: users had free access to the relatively few books stored in consoles and on shelves. Due to the books' limited quantity, their organization was of secondary importance. Medieval libraries worked just fine with inventories and directories listing all existing codices in the collection—usually just written out on blank pages in these same codices, as library historian and author Uwe Jochum has noted.[2] As collections rapidly grew, such simple inventories no longer sufficed, and at the same time, the collection's organization became more important. Inventory lists were replaced by catalogs including books' locations, which was a paradigm shift not only because the holdings were now listed in separate volumes, but also because call numbers came into use, marking the advent of an utterly new approach. The call-number system became the basis for expanded storage capabilities and library catalogs, which still to this day are of paramount importance as a research tool. Although the earliest catalogs might have merely improved only slightly upon straightforward inventory lists, today's catalogs are remarkably sophisticated, well-designed, and offer vaster research possibilities.

Organization of Shelves and Stacks

The invention of the printing press allowed for much greater book production, which resulted in a major upheaval for libraries. Their holdings grew sharply, and could no longer be stored in the library's main room for lack of space. This resulted in the creation of storage spaces designed specifically for books. Today, closed-stack libraries are quite common. One of their distinguishing features is that users have no direct access to the holdings, and the catalog—nowadays electronic, which replaced the classic card catalog—is their main research tool, relied upon by both users and staff. In closed stacks all sorts of media are organized, logically, according to not (only) content-related criteria, but also publication type and format, to guarantee an efficient use of space. Traditional organizational systems for this type of library consist of either two formal or a content-related criterion and a formal criterion grouped together, depending on the institution's holdings and chosen focus. Within the broader group—usually a system of letters—a sequential call number is assigned. To take just two institutions as examples, the central and university libraries of Lucerne cover both approaches:

Example with two formal criteria:

P.a 236

The *P* indicates media type (in this case, a periodical); the *a* indicates format (up to 18.5 cm tall); 236 is the call number.

Example with both content-related and formal criteria

A.b 1582

The *A* indicates subject area (in this case, books and libraries); the *b* indicates format (6.18–9.22 cm tall); 1582 is the call number.

The Development of Libraries

Taking each book's size and other formal criteria into account results in remarkably space-saving stacks. Depending on the size of the library, rare books, special collections, and early printed maps or other materials are stored in separate stacks, either as part of the same division or as a separate collection, onsite or offsite—wherever there is adequate infrastructure to both access and preserve the holdings.

Open Shelves and Open Stacks

Since the mid-twentieth century, libraries have increasingly returned to open-access organizational systems. This trend began in the United States, "where users feel free access is so beneficial to their work that they're not apt to give up this 'natural right.'"[3] Open-access libraries fall into two types: open stacks and open shelves.

Open stacks means users have direct access: the library catalog is still the main research tool, but then users fetch the books or other media themselves. The stacks' organization is often no different than it would be for closed stacks. In Switzerland, a few large university libraries—such as the library of the University of Basel and Zurich Central library—use this system. Newer libraries, however, such as the Rolex Learning Center at the EPF Lausanne (École Polytechnique Fédérale de Lausanne), often opt for this system as well.

In contrast, open shelves are the norm in more traditional open-access libraries: the full collection, or any part thereof, is sorted—not just by formal criteria, but by subject as well—and made accessible to onsite users. This system is especially common in libraries intended for the general public, such as city and other community libraries. In recent decades, however, open-shelf systems have come into favor for academic libraries as well. Examples include the Grimm-Zentrum in Berlin, designed by Max Dudler, where users have free access to 2 million volumes stored on open shelves; or, in Switzerland, the university library of St.Gallen or the university portion of the Zentral- und Hochschulbibliothek Lucerne, which also make a large part of their holdings freely accessible to users.

Although early open-access libraries often developed their own library-specific systems for organizing their holdings, universal classifications systems are now increasingly common.[4] The main reason is economic: on the one hand, universal systems spare individual institutions the labor of devising their own unique system; on the other hand, synergies often develop as libraries catalog their collections—and the more libraries use the same system, the stronger such synergies grow.

A Brief Digression: The Pros and Cons of Open Access in Research Libraries

The use of an open-access system entails several advantages. It allows users to examine holdings directly, an added value that is not insignificant. The second major advantage comes in the form of serendipitous discoveries: since books are organized by subject, as users look for a specific book they often find other books nearby that are pertinent to their work.

At the same time, the benefits of open-access systems are not unlimited—indeed, they run the risk of creating a false image of the library's collection, as organization by subject can give users the impression that all the library's holdings relate to the few specific subjects they come across in person. But this is misguided for several reasons. First, most academic libraries can and do make at least part of their holdings open access, but many items remain relegated to the stacks or offsite storage, and can be searched only through the catalog. Second, even in person there's no way of easily seeing what is currently out on loan, which still requires catalog consultation. Thirdly—and I believe this point is crucial—the unambiguous assignment of a book to one classification as opposed to another is not practical for interdisciplinary and many specialist departments. A book on the sociology of religion belongs in both the religion and sociology sections. Our supposedly clear orders of knowledge, the very goal of any classification, are untenable in practice. In most cases, literature on a given topic is not found in just one place, but pops up at different locations in open-access libraries.

The aforementioned reasons for using open-access systems are at least being reconsidered at many libraries. Whether a given institution should switch depends in many cases on the space and resources they have available. If there's enough space to give both users and shelves sufficient room and hire enough staff, such a system would make sense. If resources are scarce and library management must decide between hiring staff, building more workstations, and setting up an open-access system, it's my opinion that creating jobs and workstations is always preferable.

But what do such situations mean for serendipity, and how can chance discoveries be facilitated? New technologies enable new possibilities. The most obvious and most important way to encourage them is through the catalog—by definition, subject searches always yield serendipitous results, and since not only the title is given, but also the contents, flap copy, and covers are available as well, it might well be time for a post-mortem examination of the user's "natural right" to direct access when the catalog has become so advanced. Although previous iterations of library catalogs were quite user-friendly, when compared to bibliographic databases or search engines they still have huge, as-yet unrealized potential for development. Because existing technology can already lead users to serendipitous search results, dispensing with costly open-access systems could save libraries significant resources.

Conclusion

Although medieval libraries had limited holdings wherein order was of secondary importance, so they could be navigated fairly efficiently with open-access systems, the sharp increase in book production pushed those systems to their limits. The new storage and organizational model became shelves and stacks: the catalog served as a key research tool, and organizing principles now took formal criteria into account. In the latter half of the twentieth century, users' ability to directly examine certain media became more important, so many libraries made at least part of their stacks accessible or converted them to open shelves sorted by subject, creating the quintessential open-access library. But while open-access libraries offer users an added value, it is nevertheless limited. My personal viewpoint is that, in large collections where space and resources are limited, an open-access system should not be used; such libraries would be better off investing in other services—user workstations in particular.

Tobias Schelling

1 Rolf Kluth, *Die Freihandbibliothek. Zeitschrift für Bibliothekswesen und Bibliographie* (July 1960): p. 97. **2** Uwe Jochum, *Kleine Bibliotheksgeschichte, 3. verbesserte und erw. Auflage,* Stuttgart, 2007. **3** Kluth, *Freihandbibliothek,* p. 98. **4** Major standardized classification systems include Dewey Decimal Classification (DCC), Library of Congress Classification (LCC), and—for the German-speaking world—Universelle Dezimalklassifikation (DK, "Universal Decimal Classification") and Regensburger Verbundklassifikation (RVK, "Regensburg Classification").

New Orders of Knowledge around 1900

The fourth edition of *Fernschau*, the 1890 yearbook of the Mittelschweizeri-sche Geographisch-Commercielle Gesellschaft (MGCG, "Central Swiss Geo-Commercial Society"), featured an article by a man named Karl Wilhelm Bührer, library assistant and curator of the Ethnological Arts and Crafts Museum in Aarau (run by the MGCG).[1] In it, Bührer writes about notebooks and card catalogs, and adds that anyone compelled to collect a lot of notes and process them later, for whatever purpose, will soon realize that ordi-nary bound notebooks are "utterly impractical." Bührer attributes this to the fact that, because they're bound in a set order, the information on notebook pages cannot be reorganized later. As an alternative, he recommends the card catalog. "The advantage of the card catalog is that you can organize and reorganize a collated series of records at will, at any time. So if you have, for example, the titles of each individual book in a library recorded on a separate piece of paper, one title per card, it may be rearranged in alpha-betical order, or according to author name, or according to country, etc., all with the same ease."[2]

In the broader field of library science, Bührer's observations on the for-mal limitations of bound catalogs had been increasingly debated since the mid-nineteenth century. Indeed, the previously traditional bound catalog had a fundamental flaw: users could never know where to expect most of the entries, nor how many entries would be added to a single catalog page over time. The moment inevitably comes when all pages have been filled and the entire catalog must be replaced with an updated version.

The card catalog meets that exact need, and others. On principle, its individual elements remain flexible. New entries can easily be added in the appropriate places. Card indexes or files follow the same principle, and businesses were already using such systems by then, because they facilitated a much more flexible management of information than bound books ever had. The idea had long been known as a *gelehrter Zettelkas-ten* or "scholarly index card catalog," and was considered the forerunner of the bound book. In this case, the mobility of each individual card not only lets the material be regrouped and/or reorganized until it's fixed into a final form, but also enables researchers to reuse the information in other contexts.[3]

One of the basic prerequisites of these benefits is that the card file's flexible elements have a degree of uniformity. This insight—trivial only at first glance—is what Karl W. Bührer spent the rest of his life exploring. He was fascinated by the idea of a system composed of standardized cards that could be integrated with and separated from one another as required, which he believed opened up the possibility of organizing knowledge on a global scale.

Although Bührer's reflections on these issues hardly meet the demands of rigorous scientific thought, he can certainly be considered a pioneer in the field of practical information science. Despite that, he's been largely forgotten both in his homeland and abroad. He was born in 1861 in Bibern, in the canton of Schaffhausen, and died in Berlin in 1917; little else is known about him, aside from the texts published under his name. He first appears in the historical record in an 1886 issue of *Fernschau*, as author of a miscellany about library facilities and services. He went on to become library director and regular contributor to the magazine until 1897, when the Ethnological Arts and Crafts Museum could no longer keep its doors open due to financial difficulties.[4] Bührer lost his job, but continued to promote his ideas about the organization of knowledge as a consultant. Although he himself was virtually penniless, he repeatedly and successfully inspired various donors to underwrite his far-reaching, yet often short-lived projects.

In winter 1910–11, with the help of a professional writer friend, Bührer finally produced a 177-page manifesto to herald the founding of an "international institute for the organization of intellectual work." The main goal of this institute, called Die Brücke ("The Bridge," not to be confused with the expressionist artist group of the same name), was to analyze and address the mechanical components of intellectual work, thereby enabling a more rational understanding of creativity and production on a large scale. To that same end, Bührer called for the establishment of a centralized documentation office and other services to quickly and easily help researchers find the information they need.[5] Many of the ideas outlined in the manifesto no longer make much sense, and some are downright bizarre, but a few of Bührer's questions regarding orders of knowledge and how they're arranged remain valid today—in particular, his considerations on the ratio of information to its physical, media-dependent support.[6]

According to Bührer, the crux of knowledge organization is to keep all pieces of information movable and "combinable." His very first *Fernschau* article in 1890 advised that scholars and researchers include only one note or excerpt per page or card—an essential way to ensure the information collection remain sortable. This idea of consistently treating bits of information as modules comes up again in his inaugural text for Die Brücke, recast as the *Monografieprinzip* (literally "monograph principle)," indicating that one idea is written down on one piece of paper. Bührer speaks of the need for thoughts to be "fixed" as single entities, and considers bookbinders the biggest enemies of information's mobility. When a thought is bound into a book, it loses its physical mobility: "It runs the risk of remaining in this particular work, right where it's been bound, and therefore likely cannot appear elsewhere, nor be considered from a different approach, included in other works, or be placed with other pieces of information it relates to."[7]

Bührer's proposed solution for overcoming the decreased mobility of thoughts bound into book form was to divide them (back) into their constituent parts, which he referred to as "monographs." His so-called monograph principle meant that independent thoughts were to be separated from everything else, all "accessory ideas that found their way in as the author's ideas developed and were organized in book form." This separation would allow such "movably fixed" thoughts to be incorporated in all sorts of alternative approaches and other kinds of printed matter. This would also allow users—who would no longer be forced to work with finished, bound books—to freely position and assemble information in the way most relevant to their work.[8]

Somewhat immodestly, Bührer even compared his monograph principle with Gutenberg's invention of moveable type: ideas would now be as mobile as the individually cast letters that had replaced the more rigid approach of carving texts into woodblocks. Taken as a whole, these freely combinable "building blocks of knowledge" (as Bührer described his so-called monographs), would form a true "World Encyclopedia." This "Encyclopedia" he imagines not only as a serious facilitation of access to knowledge but more particularly as a proliferation of possible thoughts:

> Picture it this way: if all individual thoughts that spring from our intellect were individually printed, and individual texts were collected and stored inboxes, all of these boxes would contain a world encyclopedia of intellectual   labor, and every thought could be taken out—without being copied out again or damaging the overall work—and addressed from all possible perspectives, together with others, and be housed in collection boxes that would include these other perspectives.[9]

Clearly, by 1911, Bührer considered the library as an information system—in its manifestation as a collection of bound books—already outdated. In arguing for the ideal mobility of written sets of thoughts, he called for the library as a whole to be converted into a kind of card file. Back then, such radical ideas couldn't be implemented, but a distant echo of Bührer's ideas could be found in the boxed loose-leaf publications of the 1960s and '70s. Last but not least, Vannevar Bush's famous 1945 essay "As We May Think," deserves mention here, too: it included the first concrete description of a hypertext system, an idea that with its realization in the world wide web drastically altered the way we access information. What Bush was doing, was mainly linking the idea of a modular organization of large amounts of information with the principle of associative order.[10] We have to keep in mind that the kind of associatively constructed, individually oriented system of knowledge we got used to only became possible with the mass digitization of information and communication processes: by freeing the "fixed ideas" Bührer describes from their paper-based supports.

Philipp Messner

1 Karl W. Bührer, "Über Zettelnotizbücher und Zettelkataloge," *Fernschau* 4 (1890), pp. 190–92. **2** Ibid., 190f. **3** Markus Krajewski, *Paper Machines: About Cards & Catalogs, 1548–1929* (Cambridge, 2011). **4** Markus Schürpf (ed.), *Fernschau. Global: Ein Fotomuseum erklärt die Welt* 1885–1905 (Baden, 2006). **5** Karl W. Bührer and Adolf Saager, *Die Organisierung der geistigen Arbeit durch* Die Brücke (Ansbach, 1911). **6** For more on Die Brücke, see: Rolf Sachsse, "Das Gehirn der Welt 1912," in Peter Weibel (ed.), *Wilhelm Ostwald* (Ostfildern, 2004). **7** Bührer, *Organisierung*, p. 89. **8** Ibid., p. 119. **9** Ibid., p. 115. **10** Vannevar Bush, "As We May Think," *Atlantic Monthly* 176 (1945), pp. 101–08.

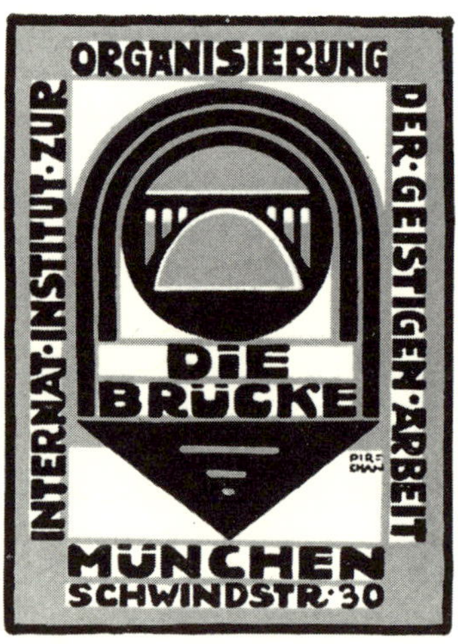

▥ Advertising stamp for Die Brücke, designed by Emil Pirchan, 1911.

2 ART

Introduction

"Therein, everything provided elsewhere in words
will also be presented to the eyes."[1]

The fascinating allure of the archive and its many secrets reveal themselves through a seemingly archaic, gestural act. In order to brush up against the miraculous, anyone hoping to access an archive must approach it slowly. This gestural act—a tedious, long-lasting, potentially cumbersome process—entails copying out a text found in the archive, line by line. The act of copying means slavishly following a template. None of the original's form is changed or corrected, spelling errors and punctuation are left exactly as they were, the source is simply accepted and carried over. The content matters little, as long as it's reproduced exactly, without too much attention; the thoughts of the copier run in tandem with the act of copying.

On the one hand, the continuous, slow movement of the writing hand allows the mind to become the simultaneous accomplice of the text's content; on the other, paralleling the progress of the hand-copied words, it allows the copier to perceive the unfamiliar as such: it's as if the hand producing an exact copy had actually come across original syllables and obsolete forms of expression through a physical act, revealing written history as a syntax of the immediate past.

Since, all too often, the intellect quickly sorts and rates what it considers of particular note from what is to be eliminated or excluded, it fails to make adequate substantive assessments and, in many cases, makes hasty decisions. To some extent, the gesture of copying a text out by hand acts as an intermediary to the intellect, leading it to grasp value directly, showing and enabling much bolder approaches to interpretation—so much so that an archive's secrets are often the first traces that lead a researcher to further explore additional value. More importantly, the archive hand-copied onto a white sheet of paper guarantees a bit of stable, calm time amid the archivolts. Copying out written text proves to be as indispensable as more free-form writing—it's on par with, and provides a basis for, other gestural and intellectual achievements. Only later, in a subsequent step, are the relevant topics excerpted for analysis and submitted to interpretation and assessment. All this calls for a lot, and sometimes hand, neck, and shoulder pain results from overuse or strain over time. But such unpleasant side effects might well be precisely what fuels the entire search and eventually helps decipher its ultimate meaning.

What I've just presented as a description of the researcher's work is, in loose translation, drawn from observations made by Arlette Farge.[2] Her introspections were first published in 1989 under the title *Le goût de l'archive*.[3] As the title suggests, they address the idea that working in and with archives requires and is in and of itself a kind of deep fondness, if not outright love. The French word *goût* in the book's title warrants special attention, as it can take on multiple meanings: delightfully, in this context, it can relate to smell as well as taste, especially as a preference or longing for something, and is perhaps best translated as an appreciation of art, implying connoisseurship. And so Farge uses this term to speak of both the archive's inherent character as well as its contents, as seen by her expert eye.

The German translation first appeared in 2011 under the title *Der Geschmack des Archivs* ("A Taste for Archives") and therefore speaks only to the archive's characteristic aspects, overlooking its contents. To some extent, the English translation published in 2013 as *The Allure of the Archives* does the same thing. This not only reduces the key double meaning of Farge's title to a single sense, but also undermines the fundamental context of its significance—namely, the vital tag-team of the archive's existence as such, paired with immanent structure and, by extension, an existing order. Even though it might not always look like it, some kind of order is invariably there!

Farge's description suggests that knowledge acquisition is only made possible by ongoing exploration. Research, in turn, means first and foremost understanding meanings, discovering shortcuts, making connections, and detecting systems, which is why the physical handling of the archive itself—actually touching materials, papers, parchments, and feeling their many forms—as well as writing about it by hand constitute its core content, while also providing the key with which to unlock it.

It may well be that the researcher still subconsciously perceives all this as pure chaos. Nonetheless, any such irregular plan—whether we choose to call it "order" or not—establishes some basic method; but what kind, exactly? And who has the right to determine what the appropriate approach is for establishing such order?

In 1994, Jacques Derrida gave a lecture in London at a colloquium titled, "Memory: The Question of Archives," echoing the idea of *Mal d'archive*.[4] With this title—even if only at first glance—he transformed the love Arlette Farge describes feeling for the archive into its near opposite, choosing instead to approach the phenomenon by emphasizing the negative: suffering and passion. The latter, as we know, also carries both positive and negative connotations. In their German edition, translators Hans-Dieter Gondek and Hans Naumann succeeded in rendering the original French in such a way as to reinforce the validity of Derrida's definition: *Dem Archiv verschrieben*

("Committed to the Archive" or "Dedicated to the Archive") captures the double meaning of the French terminology in the best possible way. Eric Prenowitz's English translation, *Archive Fever*, also aptly renders it, as "fever" can refer to illness as well as excitement. In French, *mal de* can mean both "suffering from" and feeling actual "passion for" something, so the term combines both positive and negative aspects. With the passive use of the German verb *verschrieben* both interpretations come into play, expressing the idea of having to bear something captivating, in all senses of the word.

These linguistic considerations may seem subtle, but both Farge's and Derrida's clear ambiguity toward their dealings with order and archival organization are characteristic of what ultimately remains an impossibility—namely, the goal of establishing a general order applicable to any and everything.

But let's get back to Derrida. He accompanied the printed version of the lecture with a blurb outlining his basic considerations on the "jurisdiction" of the archive: writing in 1995, at the end of the millennium, he noted that the twentieth century had been marked by incredible disasters; so, through a bit of wordplay, he remarked that there could also be a lot to say about *archives du mal*, i.e., archives of evil. Whether these archives of evil, however, are known or unknown, whether they've been displaced, concealed, or hidden—unconsciously or deliberately—is for certain authorities or certain classification systems to decide. History tells its own story as it is recorded; when archives' organization systems are set, history and the many revisionisms that follow are not necessarily foreseeable. Derrida is, therefore, of the definitive opinion that the archive should not merely be considered a neutral place of memory, a place where ideas can be traced back to their origins—in short, a place where lost time and things past can be rediscovered; rather, it is also a place of authority.

Who, though, are these authorities? Here Derrida gives us a glimpse of the original roles and rights of archivists—*archons*—who not only had to remember the law, but also had to speak it:

> [T]he meaning of 'archive,' its only meaning, comes to it from the
> Greek *arkheion*: initially a house, a domicile, an address, the residence
> of the superior magistrates, the *archons*, those who commanded.
> The citizens who thus held and signified political power were considered to possess the right to make or represent the law. On account
> of their publicly recognized authority, it is at their home, that *place*
> which is their house (private house, family house, or employee's
> house), that official documents are filed. The archons are first of all
> the documents' guardians. They do not only ensure the physical
> security of what is deposited and the substrate. They are also

accorded the hermeneutic right and competence. They have the power to interpret the archives. Entrusted to such archons, these documents in effect speak the law.[5]

Examining the original definition of the archons' task, social context immediately becomes relevant. This would imply that the discovery of an archive's contents does indeed bring back a tamed (or purportedly tamed) version of past times, but also immediately casts interpretation as a burden, a compounded responsibility—namely, how to broach the problem of handling what's in store and the attending existential questions.

Derrida therefore rightly argues that the archive "opens out of the future" and never ends, even if it was long ago left to us as an encapsulated unit, because: "The archivist produces more archive, and that is why the archive is never closed."[6]

Archives—and not just those Farge and Derrida talk about, but archives in general—are not only places of storage, they are also places of classification production, where systems of organization are devised. They are places where society and culture meet, and where the private becomes public, or at least the private encounters the public, and vice versa.

One of history's most important instances of order being created in the archive—or, in this case, the library—was the initiative launched by Gottfried van Swieten, prefect of the Austrian Imperial Library from 1777 to 1803: he methodically transformed a private library into a suitably organized public library. Hans Petschar's contribution analyzes this fundamental organizational change and chronicles the development of another special innovation—namely, the creation of the card catalog in 1780. It replaced the old inventories, compiled as fixed lists in bound books, and for the first time established a system that accounted for its own incompleteness and allowed information to be updated over time. This card catalog later became the model the revolutionary French government looked to as it reorganized the Bibliothèque Nationale de France.

Thus far, we have primarily discussed how pure language—in particular, text—is archived; let's now return to Switzerland, via the work of a man named Friedrich Staub. In 1862, Staub cofounded the *Schweizerisches Idiotikon*, which has researched and documented the German language in Switzerland from the late Middle Ages to the present day. Staub's self-imposed task dealt mainly with language-related documents, relics, and texts. But his more specific research on linguistic expressions in dialect left behind extensive documentation—we'll call it the Staub Archive. It grew to include not only manuscripts, transcripts, notes, and other printed texts, as one might expect, but also an extensive collection of pictures of all sorts: in addition to the more valuable original prints, drawings, and sketches, for example, it also included simple mass-produced graphics, plans, maps of all kinds, and even photographs.

And so, although Staub was a linguist, as he accumulated documents and analyses related to his specific field, he also ended up creating a huge, non-specialized collection: a mass of images that don't represent or even illustrate speech. Indeed, the images in question were mostly landscapes and maps of Swiss towns, as well as a sizable number of portraits, traditional costumes and uniforms, and a special sub-collection devoted strictly to folk festivals and processions, which visually documented countless Swiss customs.

With the exception of the countless bookplates in the Staub Archive—since classical bookplates often explicitly combine pictures and words—it might seem puzzling to outsiders that an archivist would choose this kind of material for the study of language, given that verbal and visual forms of language are only distant relatives of written language. The significance of combining these various media, if indeed they can be traced back to any one origin, dates back to classical antiquity and its doctrine of the seven liberal arts, or *septem artes liberales*, which were long considered the educational canon for all free men.

Beginning in the second half of the seventeenth century, Gottfried Wilhelm Leibniz became the most influential role model in terms of "creative combinations." As a true polymath, he developed systems based on connections between philosophy and the hard sciences, bringing together mathematics and physics with art. Much like Staub, Leibniz was very interested in language; one of his many initiatives, for example, called for the invention of a constructed language—a so-called *grammatica rationis*. These efforts made him aware of something fundamental—namely, that artificial language could indeed be consistent, but had no intuition. In contrast to his grammatica rationis, natural languages featured many more ambiguities and contradictions, but he also recognized that they were undeniably better at expressing basic emotions. Natural languages have a certain proximity to everyday life experience, which is why Leibniz became particularly interested in them, and was of the opinion that the words of natural languages had formed a bond with their referents: "Leibniz recognized that the natural languages constituted an entire cosmos of signs and characters that were directly connected to the things of the created world."[7]

Last but not least, this knowledge led Leibniz to develop an open affinity for the study of perception, sensory impressions, and the visual arts. As for finding a connection to the intuitive—as natural languages so effectively do—he turned to the things themselves, to examine their effect on the viewer. He considered the so-called *coup d'oeil* (roughly, "gaze" or "glance") a more trustworthy source of inspiration and knowledge than abstract language and text, or pure mathematical calculation. He defended this insight though his hypothesis of a "Theater of Nature and Art": "Playing on the gaze, at a mere glance and without requiring words, [images can] be strongly impressed upon the mind through the visual organ."[8]

According to Leibniz, the intuitive gaze requires no additional structure, it is capable of seeing everything all at once. The human ability to know and therefore act—as Farge outlines it—involves eyes and hands, speech and hearing, all the senses, and there is no thought so abstract that it cannot be accompanied by images or other visual clues.[9] Accordingly, Leibniz regarded intuition as the highest type of intellectual activity, and the classification systems based on it the most relevant. This mental construct is ultimately the basis of the cultural policies Leibniz sought to promote with his idea of a Theater of Nature and Art, from which the *Kunstkammer* and *Wunderkammer* (private art collections and cabinet of curiosities) sprang, and from which in turn the archive, library, and museum as we now know then finally emerged: "They [cabinets of art and other curiosities] represented a model-like microcosm in which the divine, instantaneous understanding of all objects and relations as intuitive acts could be glimpsed and further honed."[10] Where such cabinets or collections couldn't be assembled, or where they were inaccessible, Leibniz suggested an equivalent might be found in the so-called picture atlas, a "living library."

In the latter half of the seventeenth century, just as the major encyclopedia projects were being launched, Leibniz was an enthusiastic advocate of the idea that these reference books should set visual illustrations next to the textual entries on each subject. The kind of book learning and text-based knowledge that had sufficed up to that point was thereby nearly relegated to the status of auxiliary medium, even though it wasn't always possible to include illustrations everywhere. Furthermore, it's almost as if Leibniz had foreseen the flood of images that has arisen in the twentieth and twenty-first centuries; he was convinced that images could convey information more quickly and beautifully than texts, and therefore could offer more efficient ways of learning. Similarly, just as natural language uses certain colloquial phrases and intonations to express what is otherwise inexpressible or unspeakable, images have the ability to make the invisible visible.[11] As a concept, Leibniz's picture atlas can be considered the first iconographic archive to capture entire areas of everyday life and nature. At the same time, his systematic arrangement offers the first general schema for archiving images in an organized way.

Let us move on from the image archive intended for the public to the personal archive, where we once again find ourselves in an archive with various layers, created as an archival collection meant to simultaneously be archived by, as well as used by, its archons. Such is the case, for example, with an independent scholar whose archive is made with a specific method and target in mind, and is then creatively used and exploited to achieve specific (scientific) knowledge, whose results usually return in the form of archival materials flowing back into the archive itself. This results in an almost closed-off system of archives and cyclical archiving whose key characteristic is intentional growth in a specific direction.

In this respect, Leibniz seems to have paved the way for Aby Warburg. Dorothée Bauerle-Willert's contribution explores the circumstances in which Warburg's collection came about, its specific structures and orders, what media and visual media were collected for what purpose and rationale, and the importance they brought to and took on within the original archive. Touching upon the attentive act of discovering, recording, and looking that Arlette Farge considers the impassioned parallels of reading, writing, and thinking, Bauerle-Willert illuminates Warburg's thought processes as reflected in his atlas and library. She also explores the principle of montage that so significantly shaped his ideas of how memory works, the intellectual process by which details and heterogeneous elements are illuminated, and through which the continuum of history is repeatedly split into separate paths. Warburg's idiosyncratic vision is of the highest importance: his goal was to activate the so-called in-between space, the space between fields—what we now call the interdisciplinary realm—and use it to make or forge new connections between disparate areas and activities, however tangled or intertwined, in his atlas as well as his library.

In a closed system, *diffusion* actually reduces concentration and distinction, to the point of causing complete intermixing. The term *diffusion*, although usually used for a physical process that leads to a uniform distribution of particles and thus to the complete mixing of two or more substances, is in this case particularly well suited to describe the internal movements, actions, and transpositions within an artist's archive.

Not unlike the more scientific approach of researchers, archiving artists are already set on this (un-)systematic path so that, like their scientific colleagues, their research is exhaustive, and their results can also be artistic in the sense that they can be artwork in and of themselves, or can be the basis upon which the final artwork is created. When artists work in this way—not only creating their own images, but also dealing with the broader discourse on images—they must either start in the archives or with how collections and images are accessed, and establish basic principles for creating their own archives and classification systems, as the artist Hans Witschi has been doing for decades. In this sense, the artist can be understood as one who works to bring order to the archive as part of a production, using the subjective writing and rewriting, collecting and archiving, of (his) story to develop his own plan and individual method. He operates as an artist doing research in an ancient field, an intermediate region; his work is based on archival traditions, but at the same time he strives to make his own rules that might then allow him to throw all others out the window.

Let's go back, for a moment, to Farge's idea that the archive represents an added value: compared to the museum, the archive is granted a completely different reception, primarily because both the archivist and those consulting the archive must agree upon or at least understand its organizing principles. The individual archon and researcher both determine the particular order in which and with which they wish to explore their subject, which is to some degree also determined by the archive's content. In the museum, on the other hand, an exhibition hall's order is predetermined and the objects' interpretation already set, often over the course of years or decades. Whereas the researcher consulting the archive becomes the actual arranger of knowledge, the museum visitor must navigate an unfamiliar/predetermined order set by the curator. The so-called *surplus de l'archive*, the "added value of the archive" lies, as stated at the outset, in how it accesses the syntax of the past.

Most collections have been arranged by their previous owner or archivist in a certain order, but not always just one order—oftentimes a variety of different systems are used to reflect the syntax of the past and the nature of collecting, allowing the stored-up knowledge to develop its own momentum, so that the researchers and archons can in turn be influenced by it. Automatic processing can quash these influences, as can the banality of strictly lexical order, whereby absolutely everything is registered, without censorship and without vision. Since the archive remains invisible if it is not developed and made accessible, it doesn't have a collective witness the way the museum does. "In an enigmatic sense, which will clarify itself *perhaps*…the question of the archive is not, we repeat, a question of the past…The archive: if we want to know what that will have meant, we will only know in times to come." [12]

Susanne Bieri

1 Gottfried Wilhelm Leibniz addressed this statement to the Russian Tsar in a 1716 text outlining his idea of a picture atlas as living library. See Woldemar Guerrier, *Leibniz in seinen Beziehungen zu Russland und Peter dem Grossen* (St. Petersburg and Leipzig: Kaiserliche Akademie der Wissenschaften, 1873), p. 349 ff. See also Horst Bredekamp, *Die Fenster der Monade. Gottfried Wilhelm Leibniz' Theater der Natur und Kunst* (Berlin: Akademie, 2008), pp. 155–56. **2** Arlette Farge is a French historian and head of research at CNRS (Centre national de la recherche scientifique, France's national scientific research center). **3** Arlette Farge, *Le goût de l'archive* (Paris: Éditions du Seuil, 1997), p. 25. Published in English as *The Allure of the Archives*, trans. Thomas Scott-Railton (New Haven: Yale University Press, 2013). **4** Originally published as Jacques Derrida, *Mal d'archive. une impression freudienne* (Paris: Éditions Galilée, 1995). Published in English as *Archive Fever: A Freudian Impression*,

trans. Eric Prenowitz (Chicago: University of Chicago Press, 1998). **5** Derrida, *Archive Fever*, p. 2.
6 Ibid., p. 68. **7** Bredekamp, *Die Fenster der Monade*, p. 110. **8** Gottfried Wilhelm Leibniz, *Sämtliche
Schriften und Briefe* (Berlin: Königlich-Preußische
Akademie der Wissenschaften, n.d.), p. 1923ff.
9 Bredekamp, *Die Fenster der Monade*, pp. 13–14,
17, and 21. **10** Ibid., p. 192. **11** Ibid., p. 157. **12** Derrida,
Archive Fever, p. 36.

Aby Warburg's Library and Picture Atlas

"Two dangers threaten the universe:
order and disorder."[1]
(Paul Valéry)

In 1909, the art historian, scholar, and collector Aby Warburg opened his own cultural research library at Heilwigstraße 14 in Hamburg. This private institution was a library, a *Denkraum* ("space for thought"), and to borrow the title of a short story by Italo Calvino, a "castle of crossed destinies" open to researchers as well as the public—all of which made it a focal point for the history of ideas.

Like many private collections, Warburg's Library followed its own idiosyncratic standards and purposes. Initially created as a collection of material related to Warburg's Renaissance-era art historical studies, his interests soon spilled over into adjacent fields. Both as scholar and as collector, Warburg neither shied away from nor felt constricted by disciplinary divisions. Upon his death in 1929, the library included some 60,000 volumes: Warburg saw this as a testament to "European humankind's efforts of self-education" and its attempts to clear away all chaos while helping civilization find its true direction.[2] This collection and its ongoing rearrangement parallels the development of *Mnemosyne*, Warburg's picture atlas, a flexible configuration of (in this case) photographically captured images, tables, and image "families" used to visualize hypotheses about the development, classification, organization, and networked relationships between various cultural phenomena and eras.

The images and books gathered in the picture atlas and library are asynchronous orientation tools as well as an accumulated expression of the desire to take hold of the incomprehensible and ineffable. A breakthrough occurs in the "power of the 'undesignated roll,'" when a superior power takes form, when the nameless is named, when the designation is dealt with, pushed into the distance, without eliminating the dynamics.[3] The current status of this space for thought as an orienting condition for humankind can be read through the toolkit used to carry it out—the world is first constituted through conscious naming, putting distance between the self and the non-self, the *I* and the *not-I*. Conversely, the naming of things also constitutes the first reaching out, the first transgression of corporeal existence, opening up space for free play. This space for thought is the space between subject and object, and carries a double implication: first, the space's arrangement conditions all thought; second, the space must always be rearranged, filled up anew. The practical embodiment of an empty distance, the feeling/thinking mediation between subject and object—in which the unfamiliar threatens to "almost" come into its own, but without purging its originality—is what first shapes and distinguishes this space. "As we remove things, as we produce the space, we think: this is *I*! As we are there together, absorbed, we are mere matter: nothing."[4] As forms that embody an awareness of distance, images and books preserve the conditions and possibilities of orienting thought.

Expressive possibilities create/are space, but at the same time they preserve the original strategies for banishment and disposal that they embody at heart. Words and images are both tied down by and create their own force fields. They produce a kind of interstitial polarity—new interrelationships are constantly arising from various overlaps, correspondences, and contradictions.

The picture atlas ventures to set the stage for the cultural processing of these long-wavelength, affective energies, which harken back to the unfulfilled origin of the so-called image economy. The way the images are organized turns them into *agentes imagines* and, at the same time, highlights the turbulent search for direction, the orientation process they bear witness to.

As a form of "past turned into space," Warburg's four-story book storage unfolds on another level, embodying often reciprocal attempts at beginning the interminable process of reclaiming space for thought. Warburg's colleague Fritz Saxl described its vertical development as follows:

> The first floor contains material on the psychology of the image,
> the second floor opens with a small collection of psychological works
> including sections on psychology, symbols in general, expression,
> paleography, and facial expressions, as well as how memory functions. Then comes material on religious psychology and its unique
> issues—ecstasy, mysticism, etc.—and archival material on the
> history of religion, cosmology, the natural sciences, and philosophy.
> The third-floor materials deal with words (language, literature, the
> history and traditional transmission of classic images and iconographies). The fourth floor, finally, contains material on "action," i.e.,
> political history and the history of social forms, esp. festivals.[5]

As we advance, we come across ancient origins, advanced theory comes across the power of ancient myths. At every stage, the library acts as a "receiver for the mnemonic waves of the past,"[6] a transformer of intellectual energies, a mould and model for the dynamics of life.

The fluid leitmotif of both the library and the atlas stems from one of Warburg's fundamental questions: "How do these linguistic and visual expressions come into being, what feeling or perspective, conscious or unconscious, leads them to remain stored in the archives of memory, and are there laws by which they are suppressed and then rise again to the surface?"[7] Both *Mnemosyne* and the library are evidence of Warburg's awareness of the mnemonic system by which cultural facts function. Human memory works through montage, it edits and elaborates heterogeneous moments, tearing open the continuum of history, working with interstitial and empty spaces. Memories are elastic, and memory is not just a passive recollection of what has been, but rather the production of a new perception, its temporalization and simultaneous spatialization. And, as happens in the realm of memory, both library and atlas also create new relationships between the intertwined fields of history, illuminating transient realities. This is the structure of understanding itself, as it creates its own mobile form:

> Understanding changes, is in itself understanding differently,
> because it pertains to the sign as a sign that it has a definite meaning only for a certain time, and that even losing this meaning,
> as a 'determinate negation,' is itself once again 'of significance.'[8]

The library and atlas reflect the dual movement of signs and images amid constant editing, rearrangement, modification, and their necessary counter-movement—called for in order for the material substrate to hold them fast amid the flow of time and forgetfulness. In Warburg's "comparative historical library of symbols" the book is considered an energy storage device of sorts—a symbolic, mobile, and evocative construction that transforms worldly experience and transfers world-building energies.[9] The symbol is therefore to be seen as a pulsating unit, a dynamic memory-storage device that preserves the psychic energy of both letter and image, as well as their complex temporal linkages, keeping them accessible. In this sense, each book and every work of art is a montage of historical references and daring anachronisms, an irritating, turbulent interplay across various levels, a culture-forming network made up of different times and spaces.

In both library and picture atlas every step forward, every new idea was manifest in only temporary form in Warburg's intellectual system. The flexible order he referred to as "good neighbor policy" meant that books on the shelves, pictures on the wall, and individual images in the atlas assumed fluid arrangements; this allowed for thoughtful contemplation and the continuous exploration of new impulses—it was a device for diving into the associative flow of memory, sifting through and catching certain mental images, and hauling up their perception like valuable intellectual deposits. Analogously to this cultural process, and key to our understanding of it, researchers and observers let the latent energy of these images flare up, and learn to handle their ambivalent power. The inexhaustible combinatorial possibilities inherent in the library and atlas, the permanent process of embedding and re-embedding, hint at the temporality of all symbolic constructs. Yet at the same time our knowledge of this temporality offers the possibility of encountering and discussing ideas, feelings, situations, and views that differ from our own. As conserved in books and libraries, the past (which includes a glimpse of the future) is neither standardized nor uniform. It encompasses a wide range of historical ways of life. Many of the long since forgotten, dead, or vanquished ways go underground and live on; they exert what Benjamin termed a weak messianic power,[10] like echoes of muted voices—distant calls and invitations.

The mobile library and dynamic arrangement of individual images, pictures, and various aphorisms that accompany the atlas on the linguistic level continue to shake up our familiar thought processes. Their rotations, movements of thought, and temporary nature all expose the inconclusiveness of our thinking—which, on an expressive level, then leads to fluctuating formulations hovering somewhere "between pictorial and semiotic induction":[11] oscillations circumscribing the space of a sound mind. In both the atlas and in the library, intention and form correspond. Form arises from process, from the interminable attempt to think of a space for and of thought itself: each time an image is moved, with every different combination and each new "neighborly" arrangement of books (and pictures), a new facet is created, a new semantic field is established, and they go on to affect all following considerations, much as the links between the mental images in our memory do. Neither library nor atlas are a hierarchical system of disciplines and sciences—rather, they are a variable network of multiple (and potential) compensations, a vibrant aggregate of correspondences that produce in the viewer's/user's mind a game of connections and forking paths that impact cultural dynamics and the flexibility of memory.

Given their sheer variety and diversity, their concordance and disparity, cultural phenomena can be neither tamed nor organized, and yet the formless chaos of the void that is reality invariably harbors an entire cosmos. Warburg's twofold legacy allows him to adventurously and amusingly navigate between order and chaos, with both acting as beacons for thought—principles shaping the world's ongoing development through discovery and invention, an acceptance of chance, and the use of pure calculation. Both library and atlas oscillate between extremes, making way for a lively, vibrant "in-between space." Everything can be viewed from two sides, much as German lawyer and amateur astronomer Felix Eberty had the idea, back in 1848, that things would somehow be different if moving at the speed of light.

Eberty's seductive idea was that images from earth's past could be broadcast as rays of light and be viewed from space, as an archive; looking into this "earth-sky" would also be a journey into the past, and episodes of history would then be viewable not only in temporal succession, but side by side;

in his vision, time and space fall together (as in a museum or library, objects and texts from all periods and all continents coexist, coming together in harmony). Naturally, Eberty's bold reversal of perspective had a lot to do with the recent discovery of photography and its attendant insights into astrophotography. But Eberty took these new technologies, ventured theoretically into space, and then turned them around to look back at the earth. Instead of the telescope, he uses the microscope to (re)enter the universal. In this speculation, the sky is not a library of heavenly books whose writing lists people's deeds and misdeeds. Here, the old idea of a divinely determined world history is updated to accommodate the latest scientific knowledge, becoming a massive theater or cinema of memory in which images are the true memory-storage device of physical time: the firmament shifts from a vast, inhuman universe to instead become a huge visual memory bank of earth's past. The idea that every event is stored in this infinite archive could be considered both frightening and comforting.

Dorothée Bauerle-Willert

1 "[C]ar deux dangers ne cessent de menacer le monde: l'ordre et le désordre," from *La Crise de l'Esprit* (1919). 2 Aby Warburg, typescript of "Kulturwissenschaftliche Methode," a seminar on research methods for cultural studies, 1927/28. 3 "The desire to understand, i.e., pin down, the dynamic particular—the tendencies of our 'image economy.'" Aby Warburg, *Fragmente*. October 14, 1890. 4 Aby Warburg, 1892, quoted in Roland Kany, *Mnemosyne als Programm. Geschichte, Erinnerung und die Andacht zum Unbedeutenden im Werk von Usener, Warburg und Benjamin* (Tübingen: Niemeyer, 1987), p.147. 5 Fritz Saxl, "Die Ausdrucksgebärden der bildenden Kunst," in *Bericht über den XII. Kongress der Deutschen Gesellschaft für Psychologie in Hamburg* 12–16. (April 1931), Jena 1932, reprinted in Aby Warburg, *Ausgewählte Schriften und Würdigungen*, Dieter Wuttke and Carl Georg Heise (eds.) (Baden-Baden: Koerner, 1980), p.421. Regarding order and classification, see also Tilmann von Stockhausen, *Die Kulturwissenschaftliche Bibliothek Warburg, Architektur, Einrichtung und Organisation* (Hamburg: Dölling und Galitz, 1992), p.86ff. 6 See Aby Warburg, *Allgemeine Ideen*, entry dated May 18, 1927.

7 Aby Warburg, "Reiseerinnerungen aus dem Gebiet der Pueblo-Indianer. Materialien zur Psychologie primitiver Religiosität als Quelle logischer Verknüpfung," notes and typescript of lecture held April 21, 1924, in Kreuzlingen. 8 Josef Simon, *Philosophie des Zeichens* (Berlin: Walter de Gruyter, 1989), p.152. Published in English as *Philosophy of the Sign*, trans. George Heffernan (Albany: SUNY Press, 1995), p.151. 9 Aby Warburg, typescript for a lecture titled "Mnemosyne" held January 19, 1929, in the Bibliotheca Hertziana in Rome. 10 Walter Benjamin, "Über den Begriff von Geschichte," in *Gesammelte Schriften*, Vol. I, 2, Rolf Tiedemann and Hermann Schweppenhäuser (eds.) (Frankfurt am Main: Suhrkamp, 1974), p.694. Published in English as "Theses on the Philosophy of History" in *Iluminations*, trans. Harry Zohn (New York: Schocken, 1969). 11 Aby Warburg, *Journal VII*, 1929, reprinted in Ernst H. Gombrich, *Aby Warburg: An Intellectual Biography* (London: The Warburg Institute, 1970), p.289. [See also Christopher D. Johnson, *Memory, Metaphor, and Aby Warburg's Atlas of Images* (Ithaca, NY: Cornell University Press, 2012), p.56.]

Handbook History

Background

After moving to New York in 1989, I broadened my English vocabulary by reading the *New York Times,* and I began to systematically collect certain articles—specifically, ones about issues that affected me or aroused my interest because I had personally experienced something similar. I paid special attention to certain formulations whose concise, precise way of summing up complicated issues particularly struck me.

I called the collection *Die Krankengeschichte* ("Anamnesis"). This was a self-examination of sorts through input found in the media, and it was also a kind of psychoanalysis, with the newspaper text acting as analyst. Unlike its precursors in my earlier work, such as *Tagebuch 1974* ("Diary 1974"), which sprung from a series of personal notes, this became more of a "passive diary": the thoughts, reflections, and conclusions already existed in the newspaper articles. I didn't have to write a thing—all I had to do was find and collect it.

Biases

The unexpected effect of living in this new culture and seeing how it described things gave me a new sensibility. I began to perceive circumstances and people in a way I never had before, especially when it came to prejudices based on appearance, for example. The land of political correctness changed the way I read European newspapers.[1]

On a visual level, certain things sharply stood out to my eye: the picture editing of the *New York Times* drew my attention in with images ten times more interesting than the ones in European newspapers, such as the *Tages Anzeiger,* not to mention the *Neue Zürcher Zeitung.* Unlike in Europe, where the word comes first and foremost, in the United States, the printed image apparently takes precedence.[2]

In contrast to North American media, which gets closer to its subject matter and focuses on communication, European newspapers instead tend to emphasize corporate identity and a clean appearance, aiming to satisfy the expectations of longtime subscribers. (For example, autumn issues of such papers invariably feature at least one picture of a leafless tree in a foggy landscape). Discovering this more visual approach to image selection and cropping ultimately led to my fascination with hands as portrayed in press photos—that's how the *Handbook* got its start.

After an initial phase in which the hands from these images became the basis for drawings, as they appeared in my studies from the 1980s, I began to clip out just the hands, without any additional artistic embellishment. The *Studienbuch, 1984–1986*, in addition to my drawing practice and main focus, also dealt with a key question: What is my interest in this image— why did I choose this particular one? The accumulation of images would likely answer this question. And so the deeper meaning, the red thread stringing this collection together, remained hidden for the time being; it certainly wasn't decided in advance and surfaced only gradually, through the very act of collecting.

The Ballet of Incomprehensibility

In the newspaper photos, the shape of the hand seemed to be the least-controlled element, showing up in the most unimaginable compositions, precisely because it was never the focus of the image: it was just there. Had I commissioned photographers to portray hands, sooner or later aesthetics would've become a factor, maybe the photographer would have even decided to finely tune how the hands were lit. The images' variety and diversity would also be limited. Inevitably, the artist would aestheticize the subject, intentionally or unintentionally. But in these printed newspaper photographs, clipped primarily from the *New York Times*, something else was happening, and it was clear that here, the much overused topic of the hand recovered explosive timeliness. It became the *objet trouvé*, thus allowing an approximation to the real hand. This in turn led to a "de-popular-ization" of the photograph since I was cutting off as much of the context as possible. A kind of leveling took place, which finally created a pictorial language that was both highly personal as well as incomprehensible.

> Newspaper photographs' low resolution and lack of clearly defined focus further estranges the viewer: by distilling the three-dimensionality of the gesticulating limb into a blur and then juxtaposing it with others on a rather tight grid, these newspaper images of hands create an abstract picture of various grey tones which hardly captures the original content. Basically, the hand, as involuntarily captured in mass-produced press photos, becomes an *objet trouvé* and is inexorably included in the artist's mass archive of images, accumulated layer upon layer, and preserved in his collection of over 6,000 newspaper clippings.[3]

And so one cut-out hand after the other was now patiently placed into this space-saving collection, day after day, year after year, in a trance-like, meditative practice.

> To some extent, "the handbook" steered me away from an active compulsion to create, one which may give birth to dangerous and rash products. Finding, cutting and collecting, filing and gluing, etc. has great meditative value.What matters here is what may be mistaken for passiveness while, in fact, it is only a reverse way of looking. Hyperactivity may indeed be an unwillingness to look or a preoccupation with old images. The act of finding is quite the opposite: since I›m open, everything comes to me—reveals itself to my eyes.
>
> Of course, I'm still fundamentally adhering to my theory of deformation which has, however, evolved from my earlier point of view to now indulge in poetry and sound; it may even be likened to a poem.
> Freedom of form.
> Growth.[4]

The increasing lack of space due to my ever-growing collection forced me to constantly create more space. This was only possible by adding extra pages. One page attached to another and pages folding into each other in a snail-like manner produce, once rolled out again, those particular image bands that make up the *Handbook*.

Categories

The question of how to keep order in such a fast-growing collection was an issue from the very start. The system evolved slowly, with the exclusion of obvious categories like man/woman, work/sports, etc. Classification by size and position, young and old, skin color, etc., also wasn't an option. Using semi-biological and philosophical concepts, phenomenological categories gradually came to the fore:

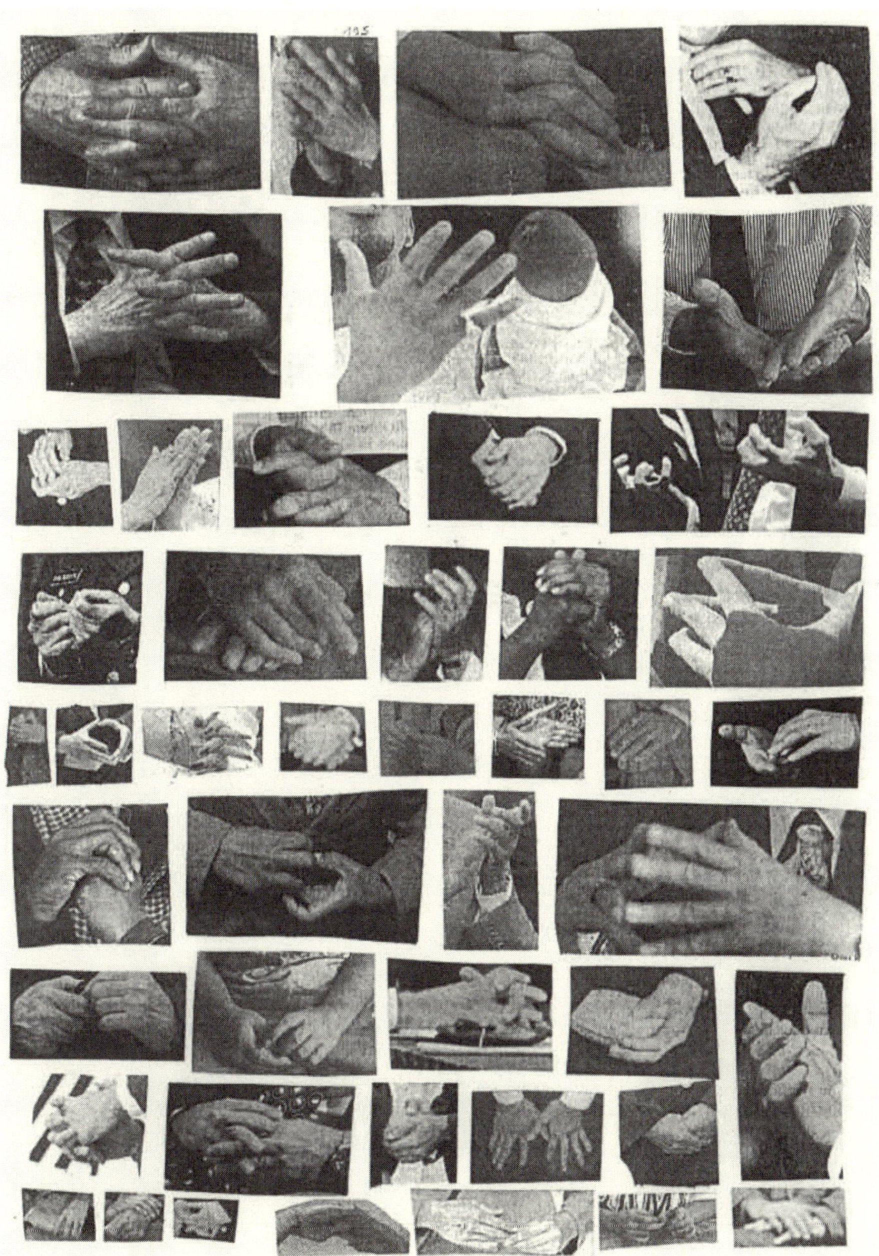

a

75

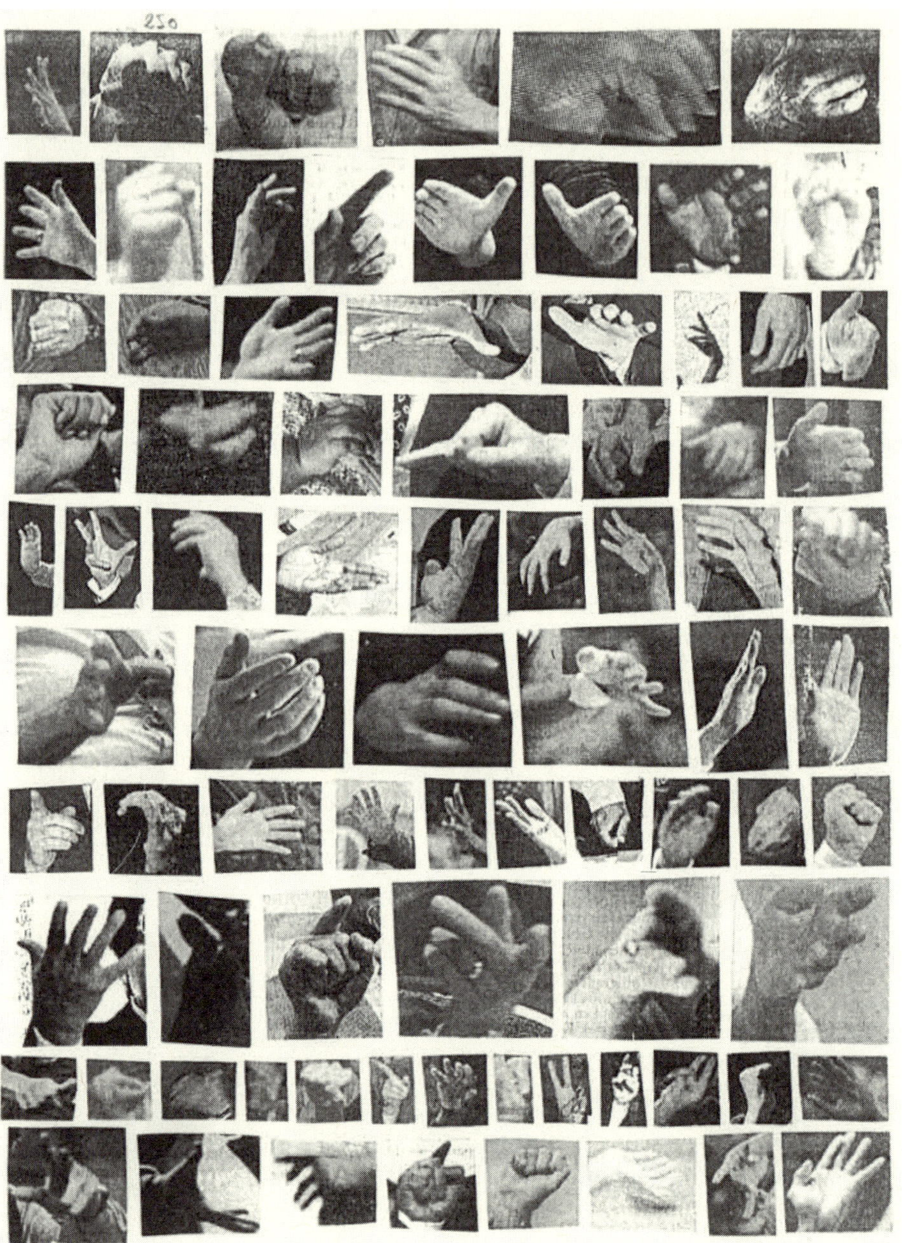

b

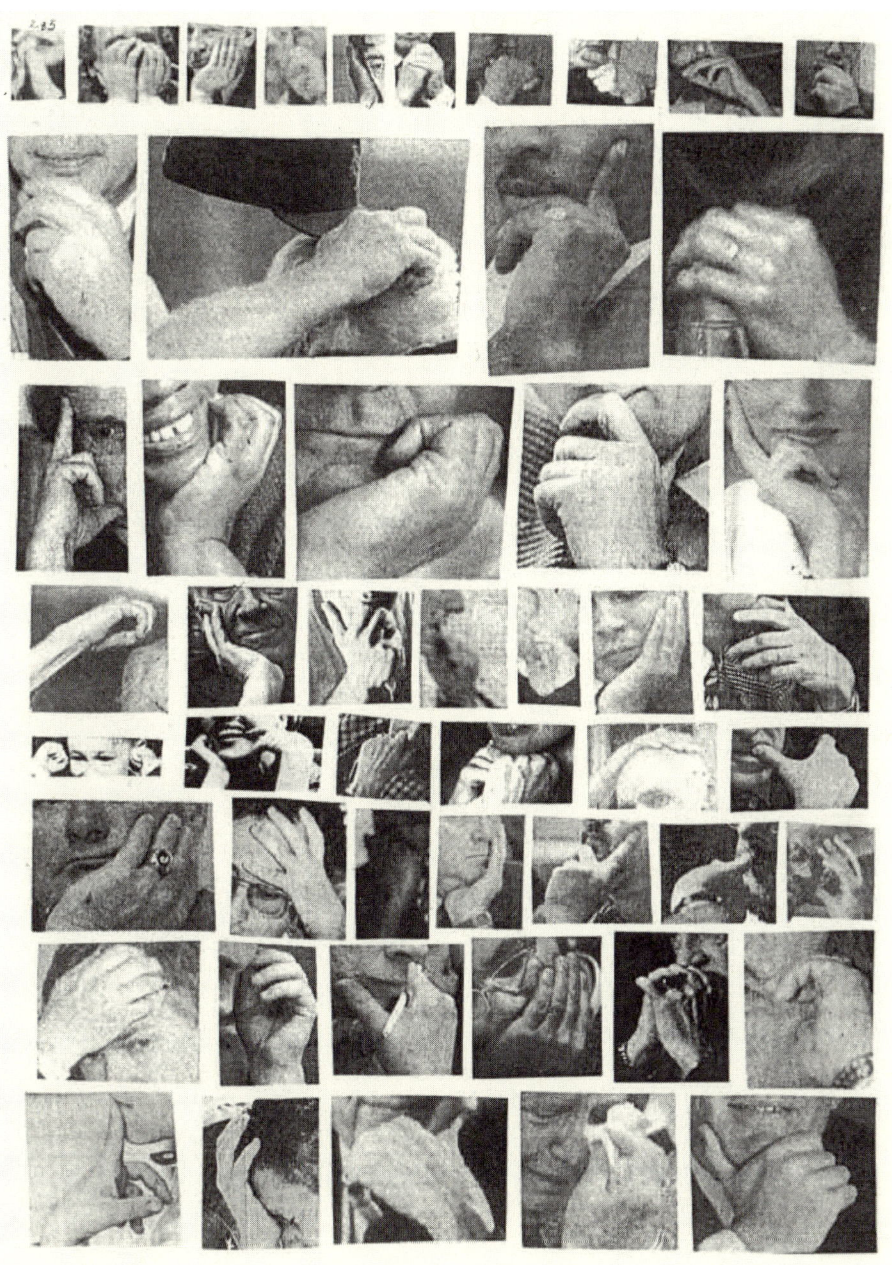

c

a The left and the right hand; the egg. b Single hand; separation. c Hand on face and head; awareness.

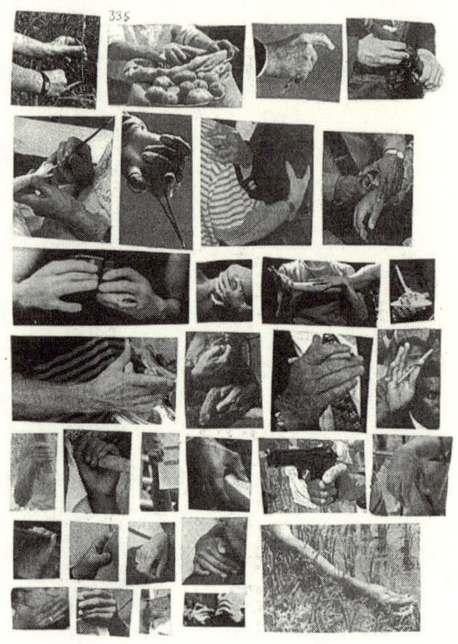

d

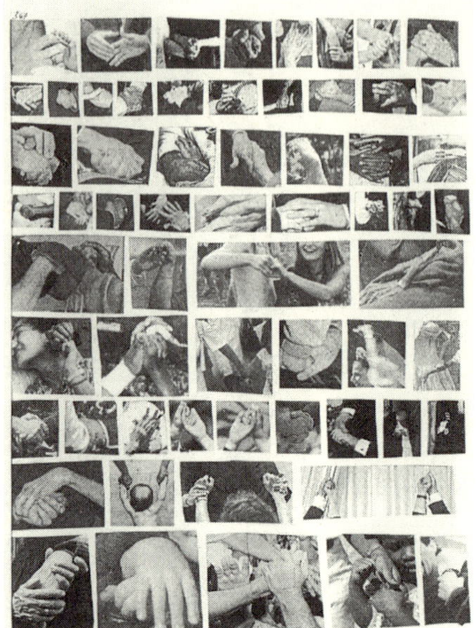

e

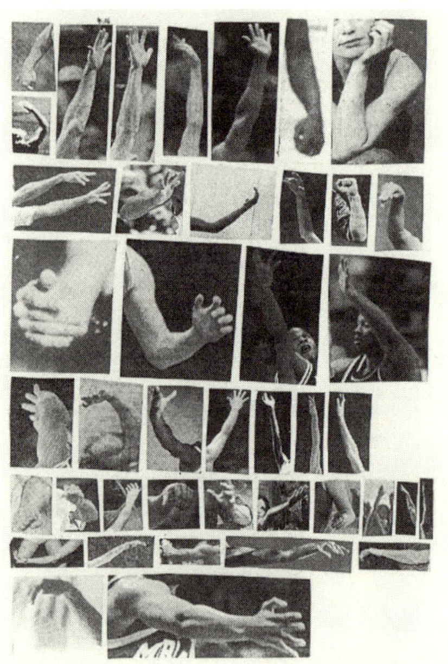

f

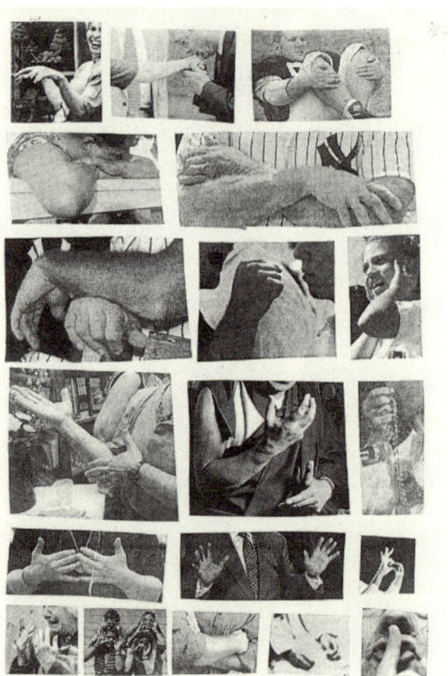

g

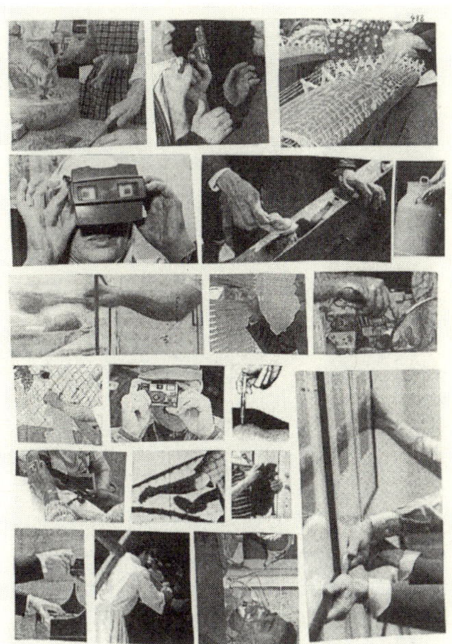

h

d Hand on object; the exterior. **e** Hand touching another hand or arm; communication. **f** Arms; growth and identity. **g** Gestures and positions; expression and subjection. **h** Activities; necessity and freedom. **i** The not-touched touch; transience and inevitability. **k** Structure of raised arms; politics.

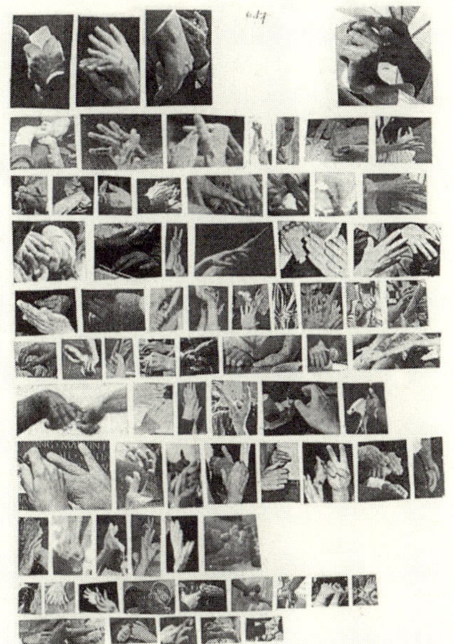

i

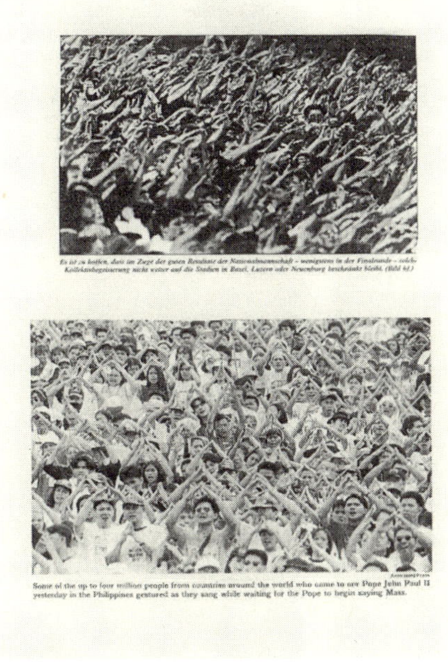

k

79

Hand to

a b c

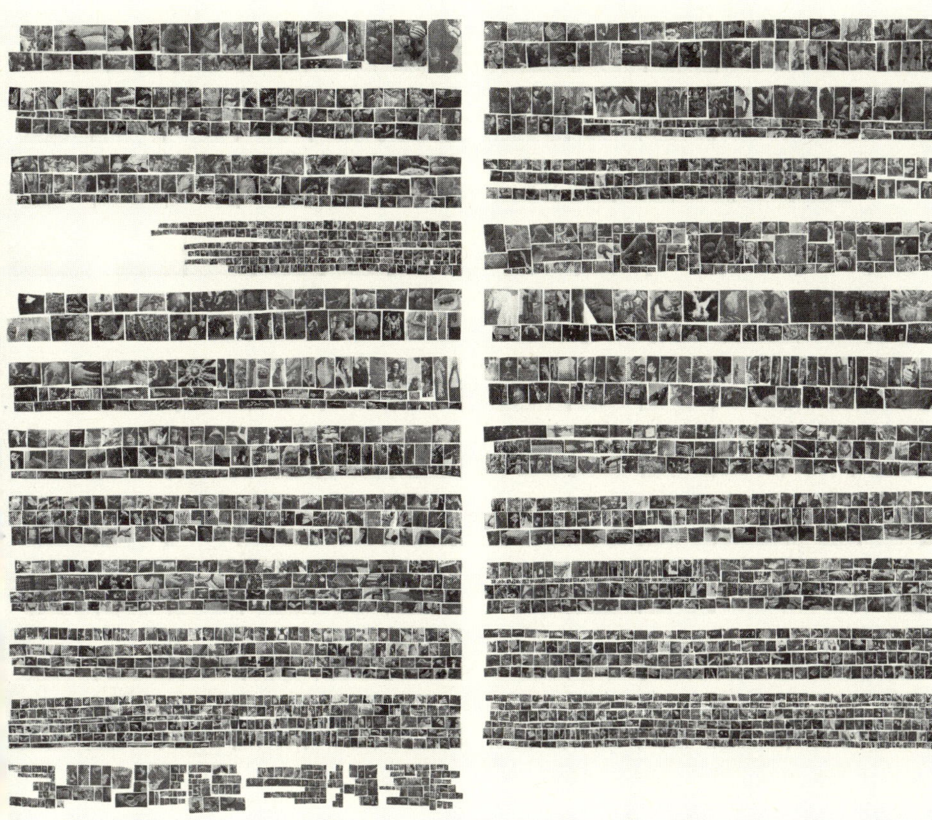

n Object

<u>f</u> <u>g</u> <u>h</u> <u>i</u>

■ The Digital Handbook.

Once the goal of extracting the image from its immediate, temporally dependent context was reached, the hands' previously unconsidered form was freed to develop further. The individual images' relation to the overall structure could be compared to the ratio of the cell to the whole organism, read as a general history of development, or as an analog to the shift of psychological perception from *I* to *We*.

A Monument to the Present Day

Time—muted and compressed into sedimentary layers of hands captured in frozen, meaningless gestures and postures, laid out in frieze-like, formal blocks set up like rows of masonry—ultimately turned the *Handbook* into a Memorial to Actuality. The collection underwent a final and irrevocable decontextualization when each image was separated from all other data, such as whom the hand(s) belonged to, publication date, and photographer's copyright.

> Friezes reading from right to left, at least in the West, have long been used to portray Christian salvation stories and other weighty narratives. From ancient cave paintings to Giotto di Bondone's frescos and Diego Rivera's murals, narrative images are a constant throughout history. In this respect, Witschi clearly thinks and acts like a traditional painter. The paintings his reputation was built upon often operate by 'pulling back from things whose meaning isn't immediately revealed.'[5]

The ring-bound *Handbook* is now in the Graphic Collection of the National Library in Bern, and was included in the 1998 exhibition *Visible: Künstlerbücher und Portfolios* ("Visible: Artists' Books and Portfolios") as well as the 2013 exhibition *Talk to the Hand* at Helmhaus, Zurich.

The Edition

I used the original copy of the *Handbook* as a template for the edition.

Expanded Versions

After buying a computer in 1997, I began transcribing data from the typewritten factsheets in the original illustrated work to electronic spreadsheets. Simultaneously, an advanced, digital form of the *Handbook* began to develop.[6] Unlike the analog version, the virtual book enabled individual components to be classified into groups—like bringing soloists together in a chorus— and an almost geological sedimentation took shape with the amassed images. Viewed as thumbnails, the individual layers can be scrolled through, explored, and then zoomed into, making for a playfully interactive approach. Seen in frieze-like format, the graphically striking overview better captures the Handbook's history—its epic-scale evolution—than if it were simply shown in a museum display case.[7]

The Self in Digital Form

The computer's rapid development soon made it possible to work on an all-encompassing digital archive. My goal was to use the simplest, most pared-down methods as a vehicle for creating work that mirrored the original, but in digital form. It had to work with the most basic, user-friendly programming, without requiring any specialized software. The solution was obvious: everything had to run in the browser.

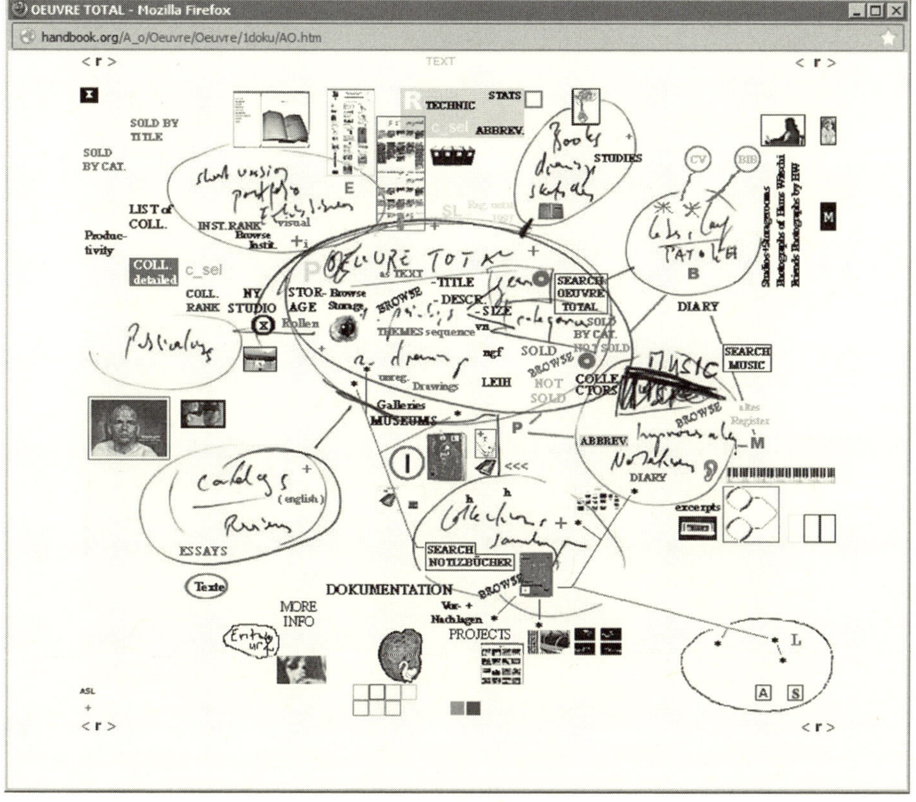

■ Oeuvre Total / www.oeuvretotal.com.

Learning by Doing

In 1997 the priority became digitally capturing the visual components of the work, which meant scanning reproductions of paintings and drawings as well as numbering the originals to correspond with their respective digital and physical storage locations. At the same time I had to learn HTML programming and lay out a design for the data's underlying IT architecture. PERL (Practical Extraction and Report Language) programming language allowed me to map the large amount of data and add a query function to the database. Sections like the bibliography, diary, preparatory templates, subsequent elaborations, and photo projects required additional processing. These main areas are subject to ongoing development in the catalog, and are the core of all related documentation.

Notebooks

The notebooks fall somewhere between a straightforward record of everyday existence and a mishmash of random musings. They act as diaries of real life and give the scribbled impression of being doodles. They notebooks include extraneous notes, scrawled thoughts, addresses, call logs, vocabulary, etc., as well as drawing studies and other work-related content.

Article Archive

Nowadays it's easy to forget how laborious it was, not so long ago, to log onto the Internet. You had to connect the computer to a telephone cable, run it through a modem, and dial up the server. Once you were connected, the line telephone was busy, so as long as you surfed the Internet you couldn't take any incoming calls or make any outgoing calls. It wasn't practical to read newspaper articles or other in-depth content online, since the line would be blocked as long as you were on it, so you had to save pictures and other files to the desktop and log out as quickly as possible in order to save time and money. Of course, once I had read the documents related to my work, I didn't delete them—I simply stored them in corresponding folders labeled "Art," "Music," "Philosophy," etc. My article archive now includes roughly 40,000 items.

Stats

- Catalogue raisonné of paintings/drawings (3,400 entries)
- Bibliography (all scanned articles)
- Digital diary (daily entries on paintings)
- Correspondence since 1989
- Photographs (90,000)
- Photo projects (*Homeless* and *Death Valley*)
- Over 1,000 short films
- Personal archive from the Art Students League of New York (aprox. 12,000 student works, materials, and notes)
- Additional collections such as *no leg* and *foreshortened arms*
- Complete archive of improvisations and compositions, MIDI files, etc.(1,500)
- The archive is fully functional both online and offline, and is equipped with a search function.
- The current amount of data is approximately 2 TB and growing.

Hans Witschi

1 For examples, see Index > Case History at <http://handbook.org/a_o_publ/history/historeye. htm.> **2** For an example, see Index > Prejudice at <http://handbook.org/a_o_publ/history/histo-reye.htm.> **3** Susanne Bieri, *Visible: Künstlerbücher und Portfolios*, exhibition catalog, Graphische Sammlung der Schweiz, Nationalbibliothek Bern, 1998. **4** From a letter to film director Paolo Poloni dated January 18, 1998. **5** Susanne Altmann, "Kunst im öffentlichen Raum: Ein Künstler buch im Internet," *Dresdner Kulturmagazin* (April 1998). <http://www.handbook.org.> **6** In 1997, the domain name, www.handbook.org, was registered, and the website, designed by Stefan Meichtry, launched. An opening event was also held at 2D Space, an exhibition venue in New York's Chelsea neighborhood run by Colombian video artist, Adriana Arenas. **7** Altmann, "Kunst im öffentlichen Raum."

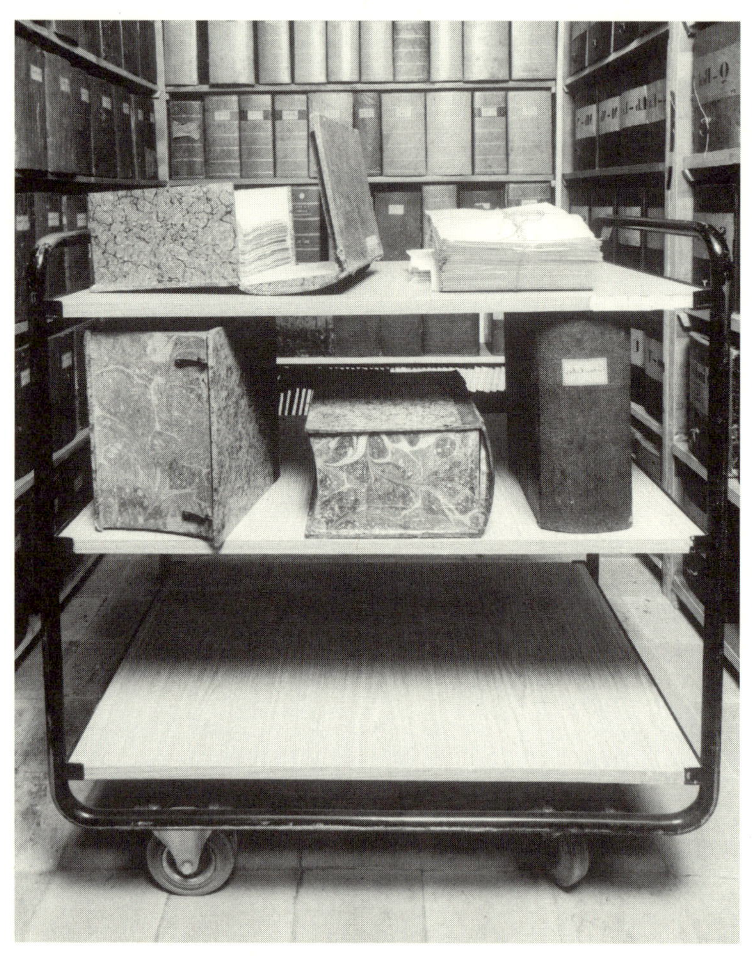

Notes on the Cataloging of Vienna's Imperial Library[1]

The idea of creating an "orderly, complete" catalog of Vienna's Imperial Library was, for many centuries, the unattainable goal of all its librarians and directors. The general cataloging process lasted quite a long time—from the sixteenth century to the twentieth—but the summer months of 1780 and 1781 marked a turning point, as a new initiative was launched to catalog the library's entire holdings. It was overseen by the prefect of Vienna's Hofbibliothek (Imperial Library), Gottfried van Swieten, who was a staunch supporter of the Enlightenment and key reformer of Austria's educational system.

Van Swieten entrusted the library's mid-level officials with the task of cataloging, while he himself tended to the overall planning and developed a procedure for how to describe each book. A detailed schedule and description protocol were drawn up by Adam Bartsch, scribe and curator of the graphic collection, who then submitted them, complete with cover letter, to the director.

On May 22, 1780, work began. In addition to the library officials, seven assistants were hired after passing an entrance exam. The assistants, four scribes, and an apprentice worked through the summer of 1780 to create the new catalog. With the help of a few external consultants on cataloging—an essential task that in previous centuries had been the domain of specialized librarians—uniform criteria for describing the books were established. Bartsch's letter to van Swieten specified that each scribe and library assistant was to have the basic script on hand at all times, so as to record the details of each book in the same manner. This was the only way to ensure a uniform catalog:

> I, for one, expect each of us to know how to record a book's title
> [and relevant description in a uniform way] because, although a
> diversity of recording methods might in and of itself be beyond
> reproach, in the end it would result in an overall disparity through-
> out the whole catalog; a set procedure will prevent the catalog
> from being unclear and guarantee that it be a credit to the collec-
> tion—created for one purpose, from one point of view, according
> to a set system.[2]

In keeping with those requirements, by the summer of 1780, 31,596 works from 27,709 volumes in the library's grand Prunksaal (State Hall) had already been cataloged. By the summer of 1781, the remaining bookcases were recorded, with a total of 23,434 volumes. This concluded the first part of the initiative, establishing a formal record for each book.

This thorough inventory of all books preserved in the State Hall, done with outside help, required a disciplined approach, well-coordinated operations, and everyone's strict compliance with a system of rules. The latter included: taking order into account—how books were arranged in the library; how they were to be removed from the bookcases; how they were to be described; how they were to be returned to the bookcases; and how their index-card catalog entries were to be sorted and alphabetized.

The initiative's second and final goal—to create a catalog based on subject matter—was never achieved nor ever pursued in earnest, although scholars were convinced of its necessity. Unlike his later colleagues and successors, who spent the entire nineteenth century dreaming it would one day become a reality, van Swieten seems to have suspected such an undertaking was utterly impossible. Swiss historian Johann Müller, who—against van Swieten's wishes—was hired as one of the library's first curators in October 1800, wrote of a dispute with the prefect in two letters to his brother. On February 7, 1801, he writes:

> Just imagine—there is no subject-based catalog of the roughly
> 250,000 books [in the Imperial Library], so no one knows what and
> how much they have on any given subject, nor what is missing, or
> what might be helpful to inquiring researchers. I have spoken to
> librarian v[an] Sw[ieten] about this, but it was in vain, and I shall not
> report his counter-arguments here, lest he become a laughing-
> stock.[3]

The historian later reconsidered his restraint of pen—"As I stroll around between bookcases containing over 200,000 books ..."[4]—and decided he simply couldn't bear the thought that all the books he might study weren't arranged in any kind of systematic order. He then announced that he himself would compile the subject-based catalog. In another letter, dated March 6, 1801, he finally laid out van Swieten's counter-arguments:

> Here, if you still care to listen, are all my superior's splendid reasons
> arguing against subject-based catalogs: no purely mathematical,
> clear division of the research fields is possible—part of one subject
> might well be considered part of another—so it is better not to or-
> ganize them systematically; it is also unnecessary, because whoso-
> ever visits the library must already know what book he wishes to

consult; and, finally, a subject-based catalog would reveal the library's deficiencies. Whereupon I reminded him, once again in vain, that although subject divisions might not necessarily be the most precise, everyone knows that books on the history of Hungary shall not be found near those dealing with pathology, nor does Terence belong under the historians of Holland; that I should be able to tell each researcher what we have pertaining to his subject; that we should keep track of gaps, in order to then fill them as our funding or special subsidies allow; that, in a word, I want to know what is in this library, if only in order to use it for personal satisfaction, etc. I am now composing a subject-based catalog for myself, for the time being, using abbreviations. Today I am up to "Bar." I shall divide this catalog into about 80 alphabetically arranged subjects. I thank God for this profession of mine, which is so inexpressibly lovely and suited to my nature, and from which I learn so much, every day, whereby I enjoy such freedom, and where everyone can see that I am completely in the right place. Dear God! Who could ever have told me, back in my youth, that I would one day manage this vast, magnificent, most august library, in great honor and good living, carrying out Your calling?[5]

From 1780 to 1820, the librarians sorted and corrected the entries in the so-called *Josefinischen Katalog* (named after Joseph II, Holy Roman Emperor, as it was created under his reign). The many cards listing works by major authors like Aristotle were tied together, and the staff then took them home and sorted them each evening. In some parts of the old catalog there are still bits of thread attached to slips that read *zu Hause zu ordnen*—"To sort at home."

Postscript

Thanks to renewed, highly rigorous cataloging efforts, by the 1960s the reading public first gained access to a portion of the material in the old handwritten card catalog, which was begun in 1848 as a continuation of the one created under Emperor Joseph II. From 1958 to 1967, library typists used electric typewriters to transcribe the handwritten entries onto new cards.

The newly transcribed catalog was set at the entrance of the renovated reading rooms in the Neue Hofburg in 1966. In the summer of 1997, the card catalog was scanned and made available in electronic form. On December 1, 1998, the physical card catalogs were removed from the library.

Since 2011, all printed matter in the library's various catalogs has been combined into a single, searchable system available both internally and externally via Internet. By 2016, thanks to a public-private partnership with Google, a large part of the library's historic book holdings will be digitized and made available online. How the digital books of the future will be sorted and organized will be left up to virtual readers, in their own virtual spaces.

Hans Petschar

1 This text is based on Hans Petschar, Ernst Strouhal, Heimo Zobernig, *Der Katalog. Ein historisches System geistiger Ordnung* (Vienna and New York: Springer, 1999). **2** Ibid., p. 28. **3** Ibid., p. 31, from Johannes von Müller, "Lebensgeschichte von ihm selbst beschrieben," in *Sämmtliche Werke* 6 (Tübingen: Johann Georg Müller, 1811), p. 432. **4** Ibid. **5** Ibid.

3 NEW ORDERS OF KNOWLEDGE

Introduction

This third and final portion of the two-day symposium was devoted to new orders of knowledge, both in theory and practice. Prior to the symposium, Anthon Astrom, Fabian Wegmüller, and Lukas Zimmer led a workshop (October 21–23, 2011) in which participants performed on-site testing of the dynamic system. The workshop's participants included: Zoë Dowlen (artist), Annett Höland (graphic designer), Lucie Kolb (artist and writer), Simone Koller (graphic designer), Julia Lütolf (manager of Sitterwerk's material archive), Hanspeter Quenzer (librarian), Marina Schütz (then manager of Sitterwerk's art library), Dagmar Varady (artist), and Nadine Wietlisbach (artist and curator). The results of the workshop were included in Astrom, Wegmüller, and Zimmer's presentation, and became a foundation for the symposium itself. Although the presentation took place at the conclusion of the symposium, it functions here as an introduction to this final section on new orders of knowledge.

Ariane Roth & Marina Schütz

New Orders of Knowledge

Traditional book structures and classification systems shape the way we think. We're rarely aware of it, but to a great extent linearity and hierarchy determine how we see the world. Although we now only rarely assume that there are universal truths, we still operate within a world of ideas and knowledge—most of it clearly organized. And while it can be infinitely useful to think in terms of categories, hierarchies, and causal chains, it can also warp our view and prevent us from picking up on other important qualities.

Take alphabetical order, for example, which follows an apparently irrefutable logic. Even though records of the first alphabetical lists date back to ancient Greek times, prefaces in seventeenth-century dictionaries still explained in great detail why such books are arranged alphabetically and how alphabetical order works. Periodically throughout history there has been significant resistance to alphabetizing things. Mortimer Adler—who was one of the people who helped develop a subject-based index for the *Encyclopaedia Britannica* in the 1980s—was convinced that we could find inner connections among the things we set out to learn, and that mere recourse to the alphabet implied a mental deterioration, a shirking of intellectual responsibility. Even if alphabetical order seems like the most natural thing in the world, it really is just one tool among many.

The vast majority of our classification systems are strongly influenced by the physical world, which forces us to decide where each object belongs. The idea of organizing our concepts without such physical restrictions is nothing new. But now, for the first time, the new infrastructure of digital technology almost imposes a paradigm shift on us. By no means does this development make traditional classification systems obsolete. They are, however, being challenged, and as they lose validity, they also lose much of their power. We believe this will lead to fundamental changes in our ideas, how we organize things, and our sense of knowledge itself. What's certain is that it goes beyond coming up with merely playful ideas: our task now is to cultivate different forms of thought, especially with regard to achieving a sustainable lifestyle, because the sheer efficiency and clarity of our ideas alone are no longer enough.

Differences Between Physical and Digital Organization

In the physical world, everything needs its own place, but in digital organization systems the place where things are saved has little to nothing in common with how they're searched for, found, or displayed. In a digital system, content can be displayed simultaneously, in a variety of contexts. As a result, such content assumes multiple identities, based on our personal needs. Digital systems require users to consciously shape the context in which they navigate. This means each user finds their own subjective guides through the system, and the links are no longer controlled solely by some authority or expert. In the digital world, we can navigate across vast distances and through subjective structures that, unlike traditional systems of order, aren't necessarily based on consensus or decree.

In this new world, it isn't possible to just passively consume permitted information. There's always the question of how personal, subjective organization systems can be fruitfully created for others. When successfully done, this results in a rich variety of knowledge. Onscreen, information can be displayed with virtually any density, size, and shape. Users can work with the information itself or with a representation of it. The area on screen can therefore be freely played with, unencumbered by physical constraints. We can create images that gradually bring information and its interrelationships into focus—thinking in images brings out qualities that aren't always easy to identify, but which often come closer to reality. The visual language of images has a way of tolerating and preserving contradictions that are otherwise smashed to pieces by spoken or written language.

Our Work

These aspects of digital classification and organization systems play an important role in our own work, which involves questioning what it means to read and write on the screen instead of on paper. We often feel that much of the digital realm still merely imitates paper, so our mission is to explore how the screen might offer new ways of representing and inspecting bodies of knowledge. We've already developed four tools—or, better yet, rules—to push farther in that direction. What they all have in common is that each questions the relationships that exist between content.

Trails was the first work to emerge from this approach. It works through a Firefox extension that allows users to recast fragmented, Internet-based reading in a more linear form, rendering visible the traces of their reading processes. It offers a simple way to transfer images and text from multi-column structures into basic, printable booklets. Trails calls into question the different qualities of fluid versus static information.

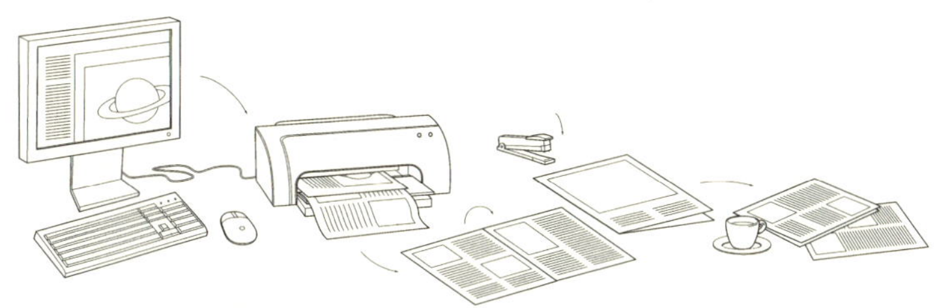

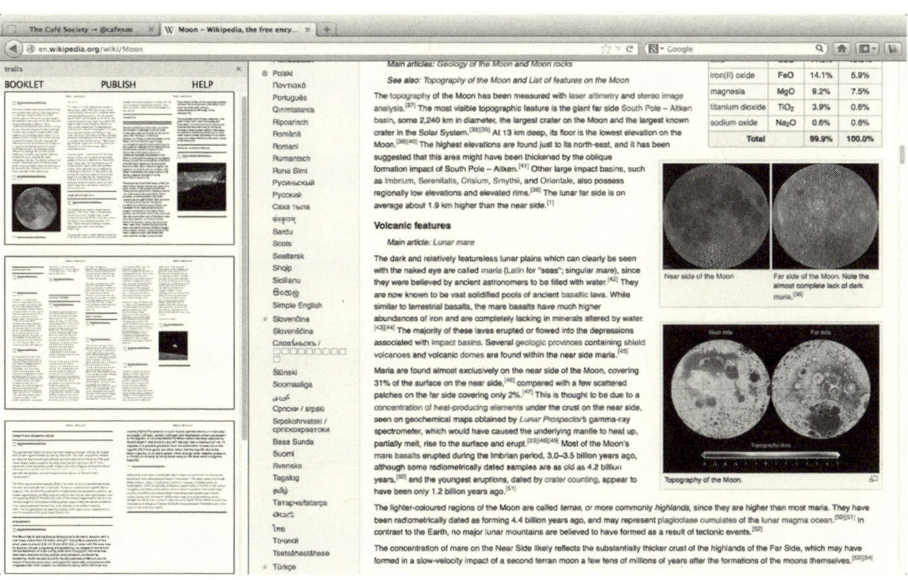

Since it's now possible to save the contents of online searches, it must also be possible to present them in a way that highlights the relationships between the collected fragments, without just resorting to a basic list. That consideration led us to create *Maps*, a platform that allows users to collaboratively present information on a map. Instead of visualizing the content in booklet form, as was the case with Trails, representations of that content are now shown on the map. Points can then be placed over any background image and set in relationship to one another.

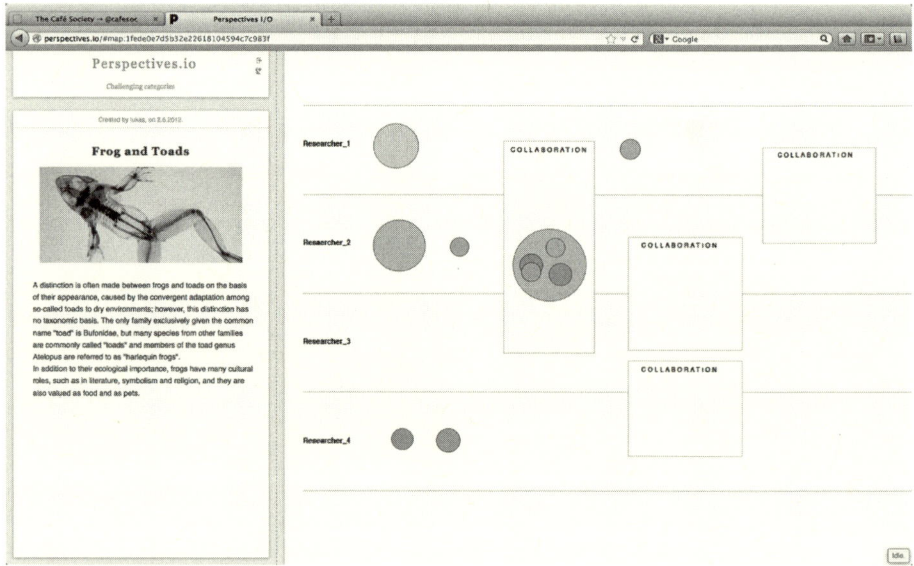

These relationships between content can be displayed in entirely new ways onscreen. For art and other creative projects, the ability to contextualize of images and texts is an everyday tool. Our next framework, *SchplitZing*, stemmed from our development of a website for an artist and curator. It consists of four fields in which volumes of content can be scrolled through. Navigation is based exclusively on the relationships between the four fields' contents, which is defined by the author of that particular SchplitZing system. Content can also be shared between different SchplitZing systems, so an image or text can appear in different contexts for different members. SchplitZing certainly makes a statement, in the sense that it's devoted to discovering the precise, quick search movements made during online navigation.

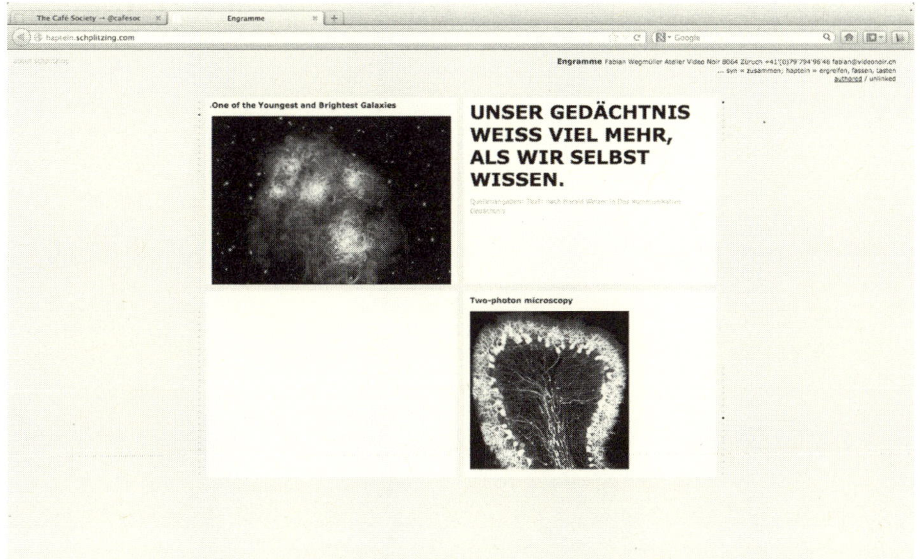

Reading on the screen has even deeper qualities and broader potential than reading a book, and yet programming environments still focus solely on the linear structure of a book—they're much like a slightly more sophisticated version of the old typewriter. In that same vein, it's worth pointing out that there have always been forms—even book forms—capable of capturing writing as a continuous, ongoing process. In monasteries of the Middle Ages books, complete with glosses, were written in multiple phases. Parts of the text were commented on or rewritten in the margins, until the book had been pushed to its limits. Now, onscreen, these surface-related limitations fall away, and with *Lines* we developed a programming environment and writing interface based on the act of annotation. The first column shows the original text as a starting point, to which various authors can respond with comments—both on the original text and, in turn, on others' comments. Each new comment level creates a new column. This means that, if you read a text fragment in the last column, it's easy to retrace the path the discussion took previously by following the corresponding contents, which are now shown in a single, united line.

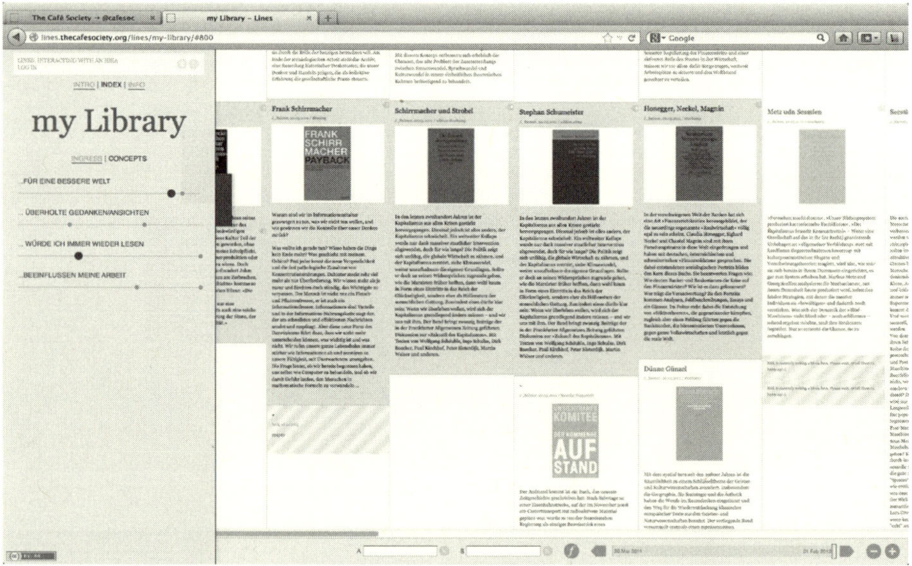

We see our works more as a basis for discussion than as completely finished tools. Whenever traditional structures of reading and writing are broken open, you inevitably discover the unexpected. But this really only happens when you can concretely use these new structures, too. This practical approach—as well as our quest to find more personal, subjective ways of representing the relationships between content—is what led us to Sitterwerk.

The Workshop

In late October 2011, we held a playful workshop at Sitterwerk where we brainstormed various scenarios for the art library and material archive. Past experience has shown that people's first reaction to the organization system at Sitterwerk—much like their first reaction to our work—is often great curiosity, and a feeling that it comes close to one's own personal thought processes. We managed to provide an entry point into these subjective, association-based systems rather quickly, but then deriving a practical use from them required a bit of rethinking, at least on a small scale. At the very start of the workshop, we tried pushing the door open and letting participants riff on existing ideas. The resulting sketches, made in a very short time, reveal three trends: the core issue in Sitterwerk's organization system centers on the relationship between its two collections—the art library and material archive. The RFID table can recognize materials as well as books, and save their basic information (bibliographic, etc.) in sets.

To some extent, in the digital domain, there's already an attempt being made to bring the books and other materials closer together. Our experience, however, shows that the gap between the two collections—the art library and the material archive—is still relatively large, and that only a few users manage to effortlessly bridge the gap between them. A group of workshop participants came up with an idea of how to bridge that gap by attaching a belly band to certain books, creating a kind of haptic link to objects in the drawers of the material archive. These connections could be curated by Sitterwerk staff to act as an intermediary between the two archives, or be automatically compiled from the database. One of the underlying considerations here is that—especially at Sitterwerk, an institution uniquely centered on the haptic—such physical connections have a very different quality than purely digital ones.

Taking the history of Sitterwerk's library—and anecdotes about Daniel Rohner in particular—as a point of departure, various participants sketched out potential ways of making the books more accessible through storytelling. Over the two-day workshop, the idea of "the Daniel-Type of Librarian" became a common phrase: for instance, when organization systems were proposed that would've brought together books about artists who didn't like one another in real life, but who perhaps had something in common, that potential dissonance immediately opens space for new stories. The key question became how to curate a narrative path through the library, and how such stories might be reconciled. For example, text or audio guides on a smartphone could facilitate shifts in perspective, particularly when two such stories intersected in a single book.

Another point of inspiration was how fundamentally fruitful an ongoing exchange between opposing systems can be. In such a system, users are constantly jumping back and forth between different positions, creating a conceptual dialogue that can be very helpful as they try to forge their own path. In this sense, it's not really about bringing the physical and digital worlds closer together—it's more about making them both equally accessible while at the same time enabling new juxtapositions.

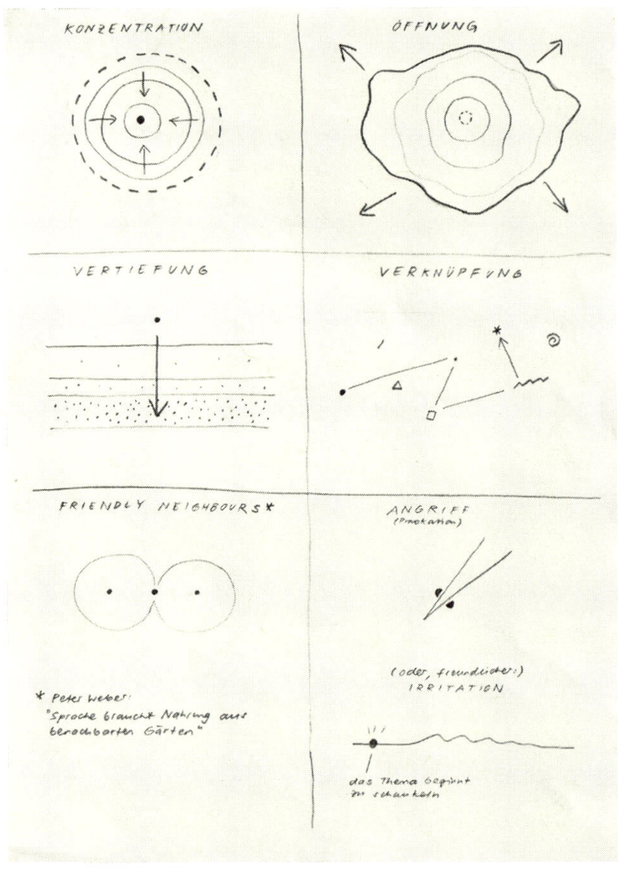

Sitterwerk

Sitterwerk is in a privileged position because its digital components were created internally, from the collection's own history, rather than imposed by external pressures. Through the work visitors do at Sitterwerk, they enjoy a strong connection to its materials and, accordingly, to its books. It has little to do with defending traditional structures, and everything to do with exploring new possibilities. This unique situation helps people research the connections between digital interfaces and the physical library much more easily than elsewhere, and to explore how these two worlds can cross-fertilize one another.

Anthon Astrom, Fabian Wegmüller, and Lukas Zimmer

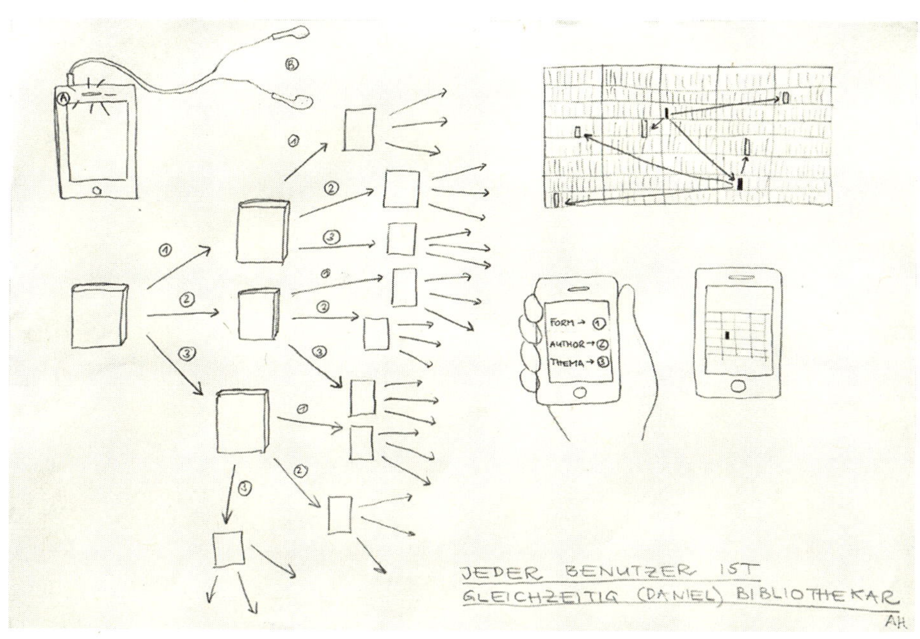

■ Workshop sketch by Simone Koller: changes—both internal and external—in systems that exist next to one another result in automatic synergies (e.g., physical vs. digital world). ■ Workshop sketch by Annett Höland: specific stories (e.g., audio guides) pave narrative paths through the art library.

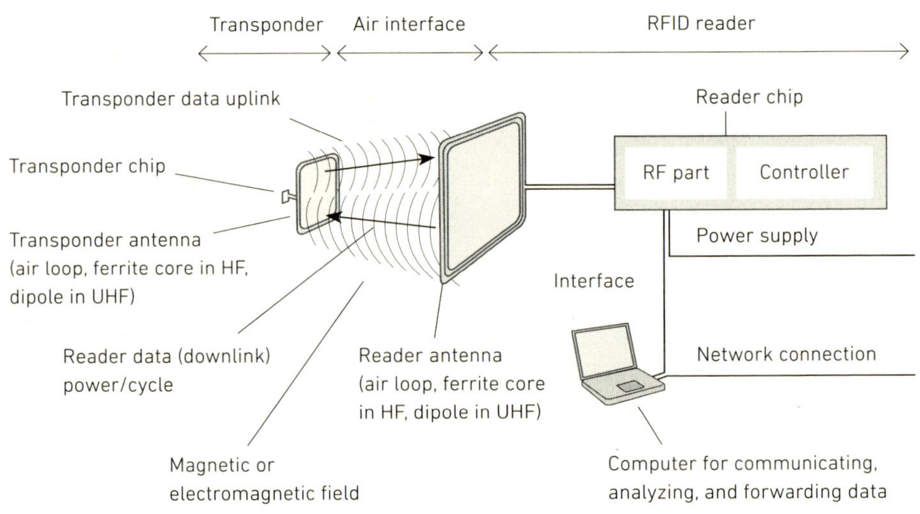

Construction of an RFID system.

RFID: Applications and Implications—
A Foundation for the Internet of Things

RFID (radio-frequency identification) has become an integral part of our lives. Now that twenty years have passed since it was first developed, anyone still unfamiliar with this technology will want to understand the basics. RFID technology has made great leaps forward in many fields, yet it remains relatively unnoticed. It is as integral to wireless communication as our cell phones, and as key to identification systems as barcodes. Most simply, an RFID system can be defined as a reader and a tag that exchange information via radio waves.

The term "RFID" is actually outdated already, even though the technology has only been around for about twenty years: the tags (transponders, Fig. 1) not only give off a radio detection signal (an ID number), but have since developed into selective data-storage media. This means, to give just one example, that you don't have to open a box—of, say, shirts or any other product—in order to check its contents; you can still "look into it" and store data related to every shirt, which makes tracking items from production to shipping to their end point of sale, much more efficient. The shirts, so to speak, know their way around, since each one knows its destination address. This 1:1 tracking extends all the way to the end customer. Such information is vital for logistics.

So, RFID isn't what it used to be: nowadays the term "RFDE," or Radio Frequency Data Exchange, would be much more accurate. Even our present-day USB flash drives might one day transmit data via contactless interfaces, as is already the case with smart cards.

The Impact of RFID Systems

Although words like animal husbandry and livestock management still conjure up the stench of old stalls, they belong to the first industry to develop and adopt RFID systems, as we now know them. The effects were significant in terms of labor management for farmers, but also in terms of the animals' behavior. Take dairy cows, for instance: they no longer have to be penned up in order to get their feed rations, and can now move freely about the barn; the automatic RFID-enabled feed system recognizes each cow and doles out their specific ration. As a result, they enjoy a much more pleasant existence and can rest, eat, socialize, and roam around the stable at will. Modern free-range livestock farms have very little in common with the old-fashioned pen setups. The impact of RFID technology was and still is significant.

At ski areas, the use of RFID has led not only to significant savings in terms of personnel, but also much greater convenience for skiers. It's now standard for skiers to carry RFID cards in their jacket, and the device recognizes them without any need for them to take the card out. These systems were introduced over a decade ago, and ski areas would no longer be economically viable without them, as efficient lift operation cannot be guaranteed without such automatic-access systems. Only occasionally do you still see skiers digging barcode tickets out of their pockets—they often only realize it as they stand at the gate, take their gloves off, and start rummaging through various pockets, as all the other skiers in line get antsy.

Similar effects can be seen in libraries: if for any reason the RFID system at the Winterthur city library is down, check-outs and returns can no longer be processed. The movement of library users through space and the interior architecture itself have also adjusted to this new technology. The library has become more of a lounge space. Even the organization of library media has changed: they are now typically grouped according to specific subject matter, with one or more subject per floor; each floor has a staff specialist available to help library users.

The list of RFID's impact goes on and on, but two points remain the most important. First, the development of RFID applications takes time—in this case, about twenty years. Second, the above-mentioned technology's economic and social impacts can rarely be foreseen to their full extent when first introduced—often, the system as a whole turns out to be much more than the sum of its parts.

RFID Applications at Sitterwerk

At Sitterwerk, all books and other library materials are identified using RFID. We considered early on how we might best keep track of all media in an organized system that could be used and rearranged by many people. The solution: taking inventory—not just every few months, but all the time. After taking many technical considerations into account, we came up with a scanner that moves along the shelves and regularly records the current position of all media. This seemed the most practical solution, and Sitterwerk has invested a great deal in this system.

In this case, the end result is, once again, greater than the sum of its parts. Users can not only search through the otherwise chaotic storage system according to media and easily locate what they're looking to find, but they can now also freely compile and document groups of books and materials that have a specific relation to one other—a detail we hadn't anticipated at the outset. Suddenly, there's no longer just one bibliography organized by author (although most avid readers still scroll through those traditional bibliographies before diving in), there's also a bibliography organized by reader—library users can make their lists available in the catalog and share them with others. This is a huge leap forward: artists can, for instance, document their preliminary research and preparatory work, making their process transparent to others. Anyone working in a similar vein or related field can use it to get oriented and better understand their colleagues' thought processes. Again, we are only at the beginning, and cannot fully grasp this technology's impact yet.

The Internet and the Future of RFID

And now for a little aside on Internet theory—because it's actually a key part of Sitterwerk's overall system. The information collected as described above is available not only within the library, but also to others outside of it, which means you don't have to be physically present to access it.

Today, we readily refer to the Internet (or World Wide Web), meaning an internet made up of information. We can call up information at incredible speeds (which, however, has little to do with quality). Working in tandem with other wireless technologies, RFID also helps us access the Internet of Things. This means we retrieve just about anything (objects, people, animals) from any place, at any time.

The next step is active control of certain processes—take shipping and logistics, for example. Theoretically, every single cup of yogurt can be tracked and reviewed, and its status can be updated. A slightly more serious application could be used in AAL—Ambient Assisted Living (which has already been installed at the HTA Luzern [Lucerne University of Applied Sciences and Arts]). With this system, retirees' environments are automatically adjusted to meet their needs: as they enter their room, the light comes on, the temperature is controlled, the fridge automatically orders the necessary food, the medicine cabinet reminds them what pills to take, etc.

RFID is destined to be forgotten, as it's merely a background technology. In the aforementioned applications, it has already been forgotten. But we must always ask what future effects RFID might have. By changing the way we operate, technology also changes the way we think. We navigate information differently today than in the past. We associate images with other dimensions, we construct new narratives, etc. This is the most exciting and most realistic aspect. RFID technology is only the catalyst.

Most of us are digital immigrants—we remember a time when there were no computers. Digital natives already make more intuitive use of computers. They will deal with knowledge differently than we do (whether that's for better or worse is another question entirely).

RFID is already paving the way from one application to the next, and will continue to do so in the coming years.[1] In Sitterwerk's art library, the Internet of Things has already become a reality for books and related materials. How this will change our thinking and the way we use books remains to be seen, but it's already clear that we've blurred the boundaries between information and things, and can now "grasp the virtual world" in ways we never could before.

Christian Kern

1 See also "Ein stiller Siegeszug," *Handelszeitung,* (October 4, 2012).

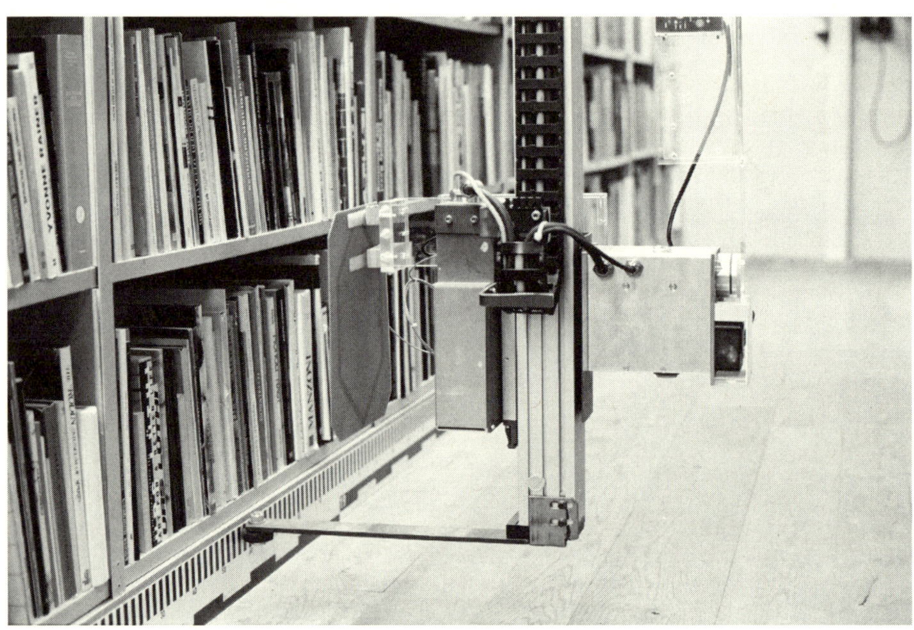

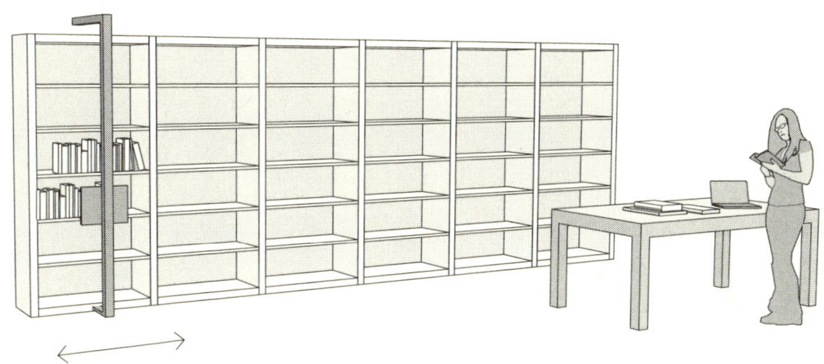

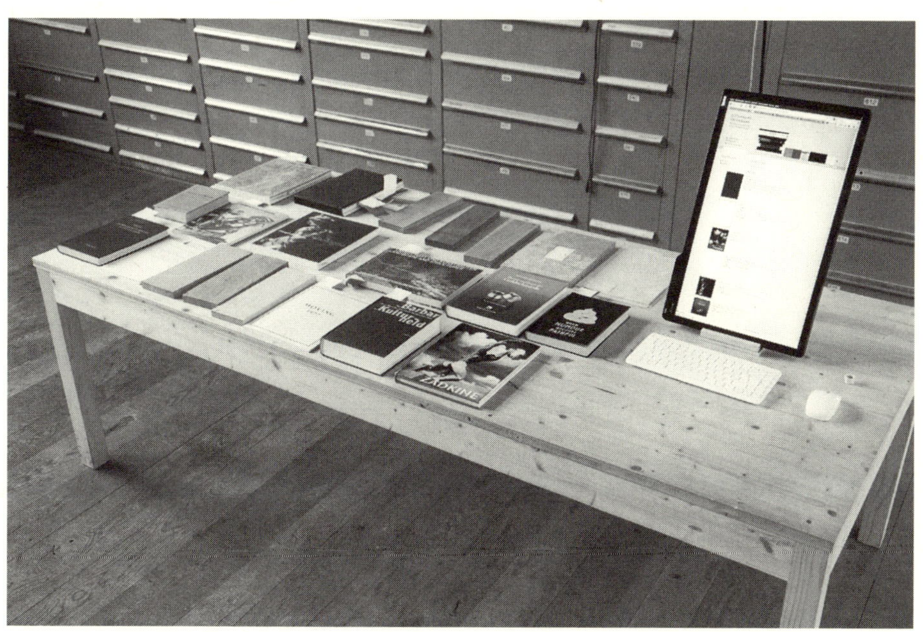

■ The reader runs along the shelves daily, recording the position of each book. ■ The first version of the RFID-equipped table, 2010.

Design Research and "Mode 2"—
Knowledge Production

Research and knowledge have become two of the most promising key concepts in design research. According to design scholar Kristina Niedderer: "Knowledge plays a vital role in our life in that it reflects how we understand the world around us and thus determines how we act upon it. In this sense, knowledge is of particular importance for designers because they act to shape our world."[1] This would seem to imply that the design of knowledge is important, as well.

This also brings the intermediate position of design—hovering somewhere between theory and practice—into the academic field of vision. Decades ago, German designer Otl Aicher stated that design theory and practice were on the rise, leading not only to a new reality, but to new insights as well.[2]

Design research, then, examines whether and how design practices might act as independent modes of knowledge production—de facto modes that are common in the academic realm yet too often absent from mainstream discourse. Several questions soon arise: How can different forms of representation—charts, graphs, models, photographs, etc.—either promote or limit the communication and distribution of knowledge?[3] What role do aesthetic experience, media-specific expertise, or technical skills play in the creation, monitoring, and standardization of "epistemic objects?"[4] Can the "genesis of knowledge" be stimulated by creative techniques, or is this merely a buzz word for some other, undifferentiated attempt at innovation?

Issues related to the sociocultural context, social relevance, and economic distribution of "creative" design knowledge production are equally important. And although research and knowledge are two of today's important keywords for design, they're not the only ones: the context of application has also become an imperative aspect of design-related research[5]—be it in the quest for socially and economically relevant research results in application-oriented "Mode 2" knowledge production[6] or under the guiding principle of a practice turn,[7] which calls for an epistemological shift in the practices of knowledge production. In light of these developments, it's worth asking how the interests of design research interact with those of society, business, and politics—and where they might coincide or collide.

This series of questions is based on the insight that the requirements for knowledge in design and design research are inextricably linked to the analysis of their materials, media, aesthetic and technological conditions, and socioeconomic contexts of use. Therefore, much as they currently tackle issues of knowledge production in scientific research, they could also address similar issues in science and technology as well as cultural studies.[8] The crux of this inquiry rests, on the one hand, on the sociocultural dimensions and contexts of such knowledge and, on the other, the concrete practices that contribute to its generation, transmission, and archiving.

Ever since actor-network theory championed the epistemological ennoblement of objects and non-human actors, people have recognized that knowledge "always takes material forms. It comes as talk, or conference presentations. Or it appears in papers, preprints or patents. Or again, it appears in the form of skills embodied in scientists and technicians."[9] Bruno Latour's term for this is immutable mobiles, referring to constant yet mobile elements that act as material carriers of knowledge (in the form of notes and sketches, for example) that ultimately improve its distribution.[10] The same holds true in the design realm: the knowledge encapsulated in designed objects can be dealt with discursively. This might enable a broader understanding of Nigel Cross's controversial design research hypothesis that design knowledge lies in design's actors, processes, and products, and is therefore best sought out in those very places.[11]

Design Turn: From Knowledge to Design

Undoubtedly such a materialistic, pragmatic reading of "knowledge" opens up new meanings for both the specific practices and procedures of designing, as well as the designed objects themselves. The core of this epistemological design analysis no longer relies on traditional design criteria like form and function. In their stead, creative practices, objects, tools, institutions, and designers themselves become the key components of a complex epistemic structure. Taken together, they constitute a kind of "knowledge-constructing machinery that turns out to be 'organized and dynamic, but only partially reflective,'" with limited ability to be understood by any one person.[12] By extension, it becomes clear that a carefully charted or otherwise well-designed path for accessing such a structure (or the highly intentional plans underlying it) can only partially succeed, and can hardly be made on the individual level.

The notion of the individual designer's unique creative "genius," notoriously perpetuated throughout design history, now stands in stark contrast with the idea of "heterogeneous engineering."[13] Instead of individual heroes, the focus now falls on the borderlines and interstitial realms of design and its "knowledge culture(s)."[14] In the field of design, knowledge is therefore to be understood first and foremost as "a process of 'heterogeneous engineering' in which bits and pieces from the social, the technical, the conceptual and the textual are fitted together, and so converted (or 'translated') into a set of equally heterogeneous scientific products."[15]

The knowledge-potential of design practices is therefore not an isolated issue pertinent solely to design research—it is also discussed in scientific and cultural research. This is particularly relevant with regard to the notion of a design turn, recently formulated by Wolfgang Schäffner as it relates to cultural studies. This design turn centers on a material-based hypothesis of cultural practices and objects that attempts to bridge the gap between theory and practice. The basic postulate is that cultural research should shift away from a purely theoretical, analytical, historical approach to instead focus on practice by examining how things are designed and actually made.[16] According to this theory of knowledge production, design—including its actors, practices, and resulting objects—plays a key role in interdisciplinary approaches shared by the humanities, the natural sciences, and engineering. The thing that unites physicists, librarians, historians, biologists, and engineers, despite their different activities, is that their knowledge-related processes all have material elements (in the form of texts, images, archives, models, patents, etc.), and are therefore designable processes.

The idea that design plays a mediating role in the creation and transfer of knowledge is by no means new, however—it was already a key part of the discourse back in the 1960s,[17] when the design methods movement sought to systematize design processes and explore their interdisciplinary potential for the production of knowledge.[18] Heated debate sprang up around the supposedly unbridgeable divide between the humanities and the natural sciences, and design was being proposed as a third form of cultural knowledge—with the hope that design and construction processes might act as intermediaries between the other two fields. It aimed not so much to define design as an act of research but, conversely, argued that research practices themselves should be understood as an act of design: "Research as it is and must be practiced, is properly considered a branch of design: (scientific) research is a subset of design, not the other way round."[19]

Looking at our present-day educational landscape, design, science, and research are once again key topics—albeit under a different banner. The standardization of higher education qualifications by the Bologna Process and institutionalization of design research at European art academies calls new attention to the relationship between design and knowledge. The most important change instituted by the Bologna Process is probably that, for the first time, the possibility of a doctoral degree in art and design is now being discussed.[20] Its implementation would not be mandatory, but such degrees often correspond to institutions' desire to protect the formal status and quality of the knowledge and skills they impart. Therefore the current discussion about design's potential as a form of knowledge seems particularly promising in light of broader historical developments, especially as they pertain to the "Mode 2" types of knowledge production postulated in the mid-1990s.

"Mode 2": A Different Approach to Knowledge Production

In the mid-1990s book *The New Production of Knowledge*, Michael Gibbons, Helga Nowotny, and several other historians and sociologists asserted that in the latter half of the twentieth century, along with traditional types of academic knowledge production (Mode 1), new types had developed that could now collectively be considered the so-called Mode 2 production of knowledge.[21] This designation aimed to codify a different approach to knowledge production—one in which the clear delineation between scientific knowledge production and other, "non-scientific" methods would steadily dissolve. Considering the current state of design research, to some extent these changes are due to the academic marginalization and methodological, thematic hybridity of such methods.[22]

The significant differences between these traditional and new modes of knowledge production must be placed within their disciplinary context. In Mode 1—i.e., traditional academic research—new knowledge was largely developed in the departmentalized context of academic interests and institutions, but knowledge production in Mode 2 is now carried out predominantly in the broader "context of application." As a result, it is both application-oriented and carried out in trans- or interdisciplinary ways. It acts as a heterogeneous, temporally and spatially flexible ensemble consisting of researchers, experts, and practitioners—many with different sets of expertise and interests—who come together to jointly tackle a specific problem.[23] In order to adequately capture knowledge production in Mode 2, it became necessary to speak not of "science" and "scientists" but, more generally, of "knowledge" and "practitioners."[24] This distinction doesn't mean that the practitioners of knowledge production in Mode 2 don't adhere to scientific standards; rather, it merely implies that they no longer need be, by definition, scientists.[25] Furthermore, in Mode 2, science and research can no longer be considered their own autonomous realm, neatly separated from "others"—i.e., the rest of society, culture, and the economy in particular. Rather, these areas have become so intertwined and interdependent that they're now virtually inextricable.[26] Knowledge production in Mode 2 is no longer an idealized practice, detached from broader social developments. In addition to being united under shared intellectual impulses, its protagonists are now especially connected (and not always voluntary) by material and economic interests.[27]

With their emphasis on the context of application, the authors of *The New Production of Knowledge* aren't solely aiming to strengthen the existing distinction between basic research and applied research. They instead make the case that in this mode even basic research becomes increasingly application-oriented, and that research should now focus on the moment of application as ubiquitous social imperative.[28] Both the application-related aspects of Mode 2 knowledge production and the heterogeneity of its collected actors, realms of expertise, and interests call for new criteria for determining what constitutes "good science." According to observations made by Gibbons, et al., the academic peer-review process might best be replaced by qualitative criteria drawn from the context of application, evaluated by judges steeped in that same context.[29]

The type of productive knowledge is, therefore, the result of a process affected by both supply and demand; defining the problem and solving it are both subject to negotiations between stakeholders. As a result, the focus on context of application and the practical nature of contemporary knowledge production carries not only social and economic implications, but also a new emphasis on social responsibility. Knowledge is understood as a socially negotiated and distributed good; the strong emphasis on context of application, however, suggests that research is also subject to economic and political agendas. In other words, knowledge production in Mode 2 carries both risks and opportunities.

Furthermore, the context of application must not be understood merely as a more market-oriented application of knowledge. Considering the aforementioned points, it also includes the entire environment in which knowledge-related issues are generated, methodologies developed, research findings disseminated, and their applications defined. Paradoxically, at the same time that the current production of knowledge is dealing more closely with social issues and problems, it also gives us reason to worry about the increasing commercialization of knowledge. Further developments in design research will inevitably call into question where each new step will land amid the ambivalent tension between designing, knowing, and producing. To put it bluntly, we cannot merely ask how design research fits into the concept of a "knowledge society" and what role it can play there in a strictly technical/utilitarian sense; we must also ask what the relationship between design and research means for design practice, and what it makes possible. The last and perhaps most urgent question is whether this relationship should be considered from a merely epistemological or economic point of view or, more broadly, as a socially based project created within a specific system of knowledge.

Claudia Mareis

1 Kristina Niedderer, "Mapping the Meaning of Knowledge," *Design Research Quarterly* 2.2 (2007): p.1. **2** Otl Aicher, *Die Welt als Entwurf* (Berlin: Ernst & Sohn, 1991), p.196. **3** For example, Michael Biggs, "The Role of the Artefact in Art and Design Research," *International Journal of Design Sciences and Technology* 10.2 (2002): pp.19–24; Boris Ewenstein and Jennifer White, "Knowledge Practices in Design: The Role of Visual Representations as 'Epistemic Objects'," *Organization Studies* 30.7 (2009): pp.7–30. **4** Niedderer, "Mapping," pp.1–13. **5** Helga Nowotny, *Es ist so. Es könnte auch anders sein. Über das veränderte Verhältnis von Wissenschaft und Gesellschaft* (Frankfurt am Main: Suhrkamp, 1999), p.50. **6** The fundamental text on the concept of "Mode 2" knowledge production: Michael Gibbons, et al., *The New Production of Knowledge: The Dynamics of Sciences and Research in Contemporary Societies* (London: Sage, 1994). **7** Theodore Schatzki, et al., *The Practice Turn in Contemporary Theory* (London: Routledge, 2001). **8** Cf.: Michel Callon, "Some elements of a sociology of translation: domestication of the scallops and the fishermen of Saint Brieuc Bay," in John Law (ed.), *Power, Action, and Belief: A New Sociology of Knowledge?* (London: Routledge Kegan & Paul, 1986), pp.196–233. Bruno Latour, "Drawing Things Together," in Michael Lynch and Steve Woolgar (eds.), *Representation in Scientific Practice* (Cambridge, MA: MIT Press, 1990), pp.19–68. Hans-Jörg Rheinberger, *Experimentalsysteme und epistemische Dinge. Eine Geschichte der Proteinsynthese im Reagenzglas* (Göttingen, 2001). Cf. also Helmar Schramm, et al. (eds.), *Bühnen des Wissens* (Berlin: Dahlem, 2003). **9** John Law, "Notes on the Theory of Actor-Network: Ordering, Strategy and Heterogeneity," *Systems Practice* 5 (1992): pp.379–93. **10** Cf. Latour, "Drawing Things Together."

11 Nigel Cross, *Designerly Ways of Knowing* (London: Springer, 2006), p.100ff. **12** Karin Knorr Cetina, *Wissenskulturen. Ein Vergleich naturwissenschaftlicher Wissensformen* (Frankfurt am Main: Suhrkamp, 2002), p.23. **13** Law, "Theory of Actor-Network." **14** Cf. Bernhard J. Dotzler and Henning Schmidgen, "Zu einer Epistemologie der Zwischenräume," in Dotzler and Schmidgen (eds.), *Parasiten und Sirenen. Zwischenräume als Orte der materiellen Wissensproduktion* (Bielefeld: Transcript, 2009), p.8. **15** Law, "Theory of Actor-Network." **16** Wolfgang Schäffner, "The Design Turn. Eine wissenschaftliche Revolution im Geiste der Gestaltung," in Claudia Mareis, Gesche Joost, Kora Kimpel (eds.), *Entwerfen, Wissen, Produzieren. Designforschung im Anwendungskontext* (Bielefeld: Transcript, 2010), pp.33–45. **17** Se also Claudia Mareis, *Design als Wissenskultur. Interferenzen zwischen Design und Wissensdiskursen seit 1960* (Bielefeld: Transcript, 2011), pp.34–54. **18** Thomas C. Mitchell, *Redefining Designing: From Form to Experience* (New York: Wiley, 1992), p.58. See also Herbert Simon, *The Sciences of the Artificial* (Cambridge, MA: MIT Press, 1996 [1969]), pp.111–38. **19** Ranulph Glanville, "Researching Design and Designing Research," *Design Issues* 15.2 (1999): p.88ff. **20** See also James Elkins (ed.), *Artists with PhDs: On the New Doctoral Degree in Studio Art* (Washington, DC: New Academia Publishing, 2009). **21** Gibbons, et al., *New Production of Knowledge*. **22** See also Mareis, *Design als Wissenskultur*, pp.55–68. **23** Cf. Gibbons, et al., *New Production of Knowledge*, pp.3–7. **24** Ibid., p.3. **25** Gerd Bender, "Einleitung," in Bender (ed.), *Neue Formen der Wissenserzeugung* (Frankfurt am Main: Campus, 2001), p.11. **26** Gibbons et al., *New Production of Knowledge*, p.9. **27** Ibid., p.155. **28** Nowotny, *Es ist so*, p.50. **29** Gibbons, et al., *New Production of Knowledge*, p.9.

Contributors

Anthon Astrom (b. 1983) studied the natural sciences and fine arts. Since 2002, he has been a university lecturer, programmer, and designer; since 2009, he has worked at the Woods, Zürich. In 2011, Astrom and Lukas Zimmer cofounded the design studio Astrom/Zimmer.

Dorothée Bauerle-Willert (b. 1951), PhD, studied art history, literature, and philosophy in Tübingen and Marburg. In 1977, she was research associate at the Warburg Institute in London, and in 1980, she completed her doctorate. From 1980 to 1983, she was research assistant at the Staatliche Kunsthalle Baden-Baden; also in 1983, she became director of the Gesellschaft für Aktuelle Kunst (Society for Contemporary Art) in Bremen, and from 1983 to 1990, she served as deputy director at the Ulmer Museum. From 1990 to 2007, she was visiting professor of literature and art history at universities in Asunción, Paraguay; Montevideo, Uruguay; Tallinn, Estonia; Skopje, Macedonia; and Belgrade, Serbia.

Since February 2007, she has been a freelance writer based in Berlin, in addition to teaching at the Universität zu Köln (University of Cologne), the Hochschule der Künste (Academy of Fine Arts) Dresden, and the Hochschule für Kunst und Design (Academy of Art and Design) Halle. Since January 2010, she has also been guest dramaturge at the Vorarlberger Landestheater (Vorarlberg State Theatre) in Bregenz. She has published several works on contemporary art.

Susanne Bieri (b. 1960), PhD, is an art historian. As director of the Prints and Drawings Department of the Swiss National Library, she also manages its Special Collections and Federal Historic Monument Archive. She is president of the CCSA (Catalogue collectif des affiches suisses/Swiss Poster Catalog), Memoriav (an association for the preservation of Switzerland's audiovisual heritage), and the Kantonalen Kunstkommission Bern (Cantonal Art Committee); she is also vice-president of the advisory board of m.a.x. museo, Chiasso. Bieri is a member of the Sitterwerk Foundation, St. Gallen, and serves on the advisory board of its art library. She has produced numerous publications, art editions/artists' books, and exhibitions dealing with the history of the Prints and Drawings Department at the Swiss National library, and has overseen the acquisition of several major artists' archives (Daniel Spoerri, Karl Gerstner, Johannes Gachnang, Ulrich Meister, et al.). She recently completed a doctorate in art history at the University of Basel with Andreas Beyer ("Image and Library: The Prints and Drawings Department of the Swiss National Library or How Art Entered the Library and Why it Stayed").

Christian Kern (b.1961), ScD, studied agriculture and received his PhD from the Technische Universität München (Technical University of Munich) in 1997, with a dissertation on the use of RFID in animal husbandry. He has worked in R&D for the semiconductor industry, and has done extensive research for the Bavarian Ministry of Business and the Environment. In 1998, he began working in the paper industry, and soon after founded a company that manages the use of RFID in several Swiss libraries. In 2004, he founded InfoMedis AG, a company specializing in RFID system software middleware for process control and patient record tracking in hospitals, as well as for various applications in libraries, museums, and office archives (including the art library at Sitterwerk). Kern is the author of two books, works as an appraiser, serves on several industrial standardization committees, and is also president of the Swiss Smart Card Forum.

Felix Lehner (b.1960) trained as a bookseller before fully devoting his time to sculpture and the craft of foundry casting. In 1983, he established his own art foundry in Beinwil am See, and in 1994, moved it to St.Gallen. He has overseen the foundry's steady growth ever since, and continues to manage its everyday operation. In 2006—alongside architect Hans Jörg Schmid, owner of the former dyeworks, and book collector Daniel Rohner— he cofounded the Sitterwerk Foundation, a non-profit organization devoted to the development and research of art.

Claudia Mareis (b.1974), PhD, is a designer, as well as professor of design theory and history. Since February 2013, she has served as director of the Institute for Experimental Design and Media Cultures at the Academy of Art and Design Basel. From 2010 to 2013, she participated in the Image, Model, Design research group of the Iconic Criticism/eikones project—an initiative of the NCCR (National Centres of Competence in Research), conducted under the aegis of the NFS (Swiss National Science Foundation) at the University of Basel—and completed her post-doc on the history and practice of creativity and idea-generation techniques in the postwar period. Mareis has taught design theory and history at several universities in Switzerland and Germany, including the University of Basel (2015), Vilnius Academy of Arts (2014), Zurich University of the Arts (2011–13), Bern University of the Arts

(2006–13), Humboldt University Berlin (2011), and Berlin University of the Arts (2013). She completed her doctorate in 2010, and her dissertation was subsequently published as *Design als Wissenskultur* ("Design as Epistemic Culture") (Bielefeld: Transcript Verlag, 2011). She is a board member of DGTF (Deutsche Gesellschaft für Designtheorie und -forschung, the German Society for Design Theory and Research) and member of Birkhäuser Verlag's BIRD (Board of International Research in Design).

Gerhard W. Matter (b.1955), PhD, studied history and geography at the University of Zurich, where he also completed a doctorate in constitutional history. He trained as a scientific librarian in Zurich and Toronto, and since 2005, has been director of the Kantonsbibliothek Baselland (cantonal library) in Liestal. A lecturer at the University of Zurich, he has been an active proponent of library science education for several years. He serves on the advisory board of the IT department at the University of Chur, as well as the German professional journal *Buch und Bibliothek* ("Books and Libraries").

Philipp Messner (b.1975), MA, studied cultural sciences at Humboldt University Berlin and holds a postgraduate degree in archival, library, and information science. He works as an archivist at the University of Zurich. He is interested primarily in the material and media-related aspects of how knowledge and social memory are organized.

Paul Michel (b.1947), PhD, studied German literature and art history from 1965 to 1972 at the Universities of Zurich and Münster/Westphalia. He completed his doctorate in 1976, and in 1986, finished his post-doc in German philology from the Middle Ages to the early modern period. From 1985 to 1989, he taught German at the Kantonsschule Zürcher Unterland grammar school in Bülach. He began teaching at the University of Zurich during the 1989–90 winter semester, and stayed on as professor emeritus after taking early retirement in 2007. His research focuses on the history of early exegesis (including an NFS project with Hans Weder and several publications coauthored with Regula Forster), encyclopedias (including a research project with Madeleine Herren and publication coauthored with Martin Rüesch), physicotheology, allegory, and the visualization of knowledge. See also www.enzyklopaedie.ch.

Hans Petschar (b.1959), PhD, studied history and German philology at the University of Salzburg, where he completed his doctorate in 1985. He has led several projects for the digitization of cultural heritage at the Österreichische Nationalbibliothek (Austrian National Library), where he was appointed director of the Picture Archives and Graphics Department in 2002.

Since 2002, Petschar has served as the Austrian National Library's official representative at CENL (the Conference of European National Librarians). He has produced several publications on the history of books and libraries, as well as media history and Austrian history.

Alta L. Price (b.1980) runs an editorial consultancy specialized in literature and nonfiction texts on art, architecture, design, and culture. She translates from Italian and German into English, and was awarded the 2013 Gutekunst Prize. Her most recent publications include books by Corrado Augias and illustrator Beppe Giacobbe, as well as short stories by Gabriele Pedullà. Her translation of a landmark publication on Weimar-era editorial design is forthcoming from Taschen. She has also contributed to journals including *3 Quarks Daily*, *Candide*, *Log*, the *IAPMA Bulletin*, *Codex: The Journal of Letter-forms*, and *Progetto grafico*. She is vice-president of the New York Circle of Translators, and is also a member of the PEN American Center Translation Committee.

Ariane Roth (b.1980) holds a design degree, and has been manager of the Sitterwerk Foundation since 2010. After studying photography in Germany, she went on to oversee the estate of Zurich-based photographer Andreas Züst, and as project manager of his library she organized a traveling exhibition titled *Von Andreas bis Züst – eine Bibliothek auf Wanderschaft, 2009–2010* ("From Andreas to Züst: A Library on the Move, 2009–2010"), which was also shown at Sitterwerk. In 2009, she completed a part-time master's degree in cultural management at the Universität Basel (University of Basel).

Tobias Schelling (b.1976), MA, trained as a librarian and earned a bachelor's degree in documentation and information science. He went on to work at various academic libraries, and studied anthropology at the Universities of Zurich and Basel. He served as project manager of various construction projects at the Zentral- und Hochschulbibliothek Luzern (Central/University Library of Lucerne) and the GGG Stadtbibliothek Basel (City Library of the Gesellschaft für das Gute und Gemeinnützige, "Society for the Good and Charitable") in 2014 and 2015, respectively. Currently, he is a library administrator for the Canton of Zurich, working as a consultant to public libraries.

Marina Schütz (b.1956), MA, initially completed a primary-school teaching certificate before going on to work in the book trade, where she gained many years of experience with art and artists' books. She studied art history, film, and contemporary German literature in Zurich. She managed Sitterwerk's art library from 2006 to 2014, and in September 2014, became program director for the Kinok Cinema, part of the Lokremise Cultural Center in St.Gallen.

Fabian Wegmüller (b.1982) helped cofound the Woods, after studying in the video department of the Hochschule Luzern Kunst und Design (Lucerne School of Art and Design). He works as a freelance filmmaker and collaborates with Astrom/Zimmer on projects combining art, design, and research. He also works with videocompany, a production company in Zurich, as video technician for various art projects and exhibitions.

Hans Witschi (b.1954) studied painting in Zurich under Gustav Guldener in the 1970s. He moved to New York City in 1989, after receiving the Studio Grant from the City of Zurich. Witschi's work has been shown at Shedhalle, Zurich; Kunsthalle Palazzo, Basel; Kunsthistorisches Museum Schloss Ambras, Innsbruck; Andrea Robbi Museum in Sils-Maria, as part of the annual St. Moritz Art Masters (SAM); Ursus Books; On Stellar Rays; and VOLTA NY (2014). His work is held in numerous collections including Rockefeller University; the Graphic Collection of the National Library, Bern, Switzerland; and the Musée d'art et d'histoire de la Ville de Neuchatel. Paolo Poloni's documentary on Witschi's life, *Witschi geht*, was shown at the Locarno Film Festival in 1992, the same year Witschi received the Federal Visual Art Fellowship of Switzerland. Witschi's collaborations with other artists range from piano music for Noritoshi Hirakawa's video, "A Destination of Ego," at PS.1 (1994) to performances with Bruno Jakob at the Kunstmuseum Lucerne (2012) and Kolumba Cologne (2014); in 2011, the Glassfarm Ensemble premiered his *OCULUS* at the Stone. *Hans Witschi*, a comprehensive monograph, was published in 2012; in December 2013, a lengthy interview conducted by Zipora Fried appeared in *BOMB Magazine*.

Lukas Zimmer (b.1980) studied visual communication in Bern and at Rietveld Academy Amsterdam. He is involved in research projects at various universities, and, since 2007, he has been a freelance graphic artist, based in the Woods, Zürich. In 2011, he founded Astrom/Zimmer, together with Anthon Astrom.

The Dynamic Library: Organizing Knowledge at the Sitterwerk—Precedents and Possibilities was first published in 2015 by Soberscove Press.

Design: István Scheibler
Lithography: Henrik Strömberg
Editiorial assistance: Vanessa Simili

Print Run: 1250
Library of Congress Control Number: 2015941263
ISBN: 978-1-940190-09-9

The Dynamic Library was made possible with the support of the Swiss Arts Council Pro Helvetia.

www.soberscove.com

Archive der Zukunft: Neue Wissensordnungen im Sitterwerk was first published in 2013 by Stiftung Sitterwerk St.Gallen.

The 2011 *Archive der Zukunft* symposium and workshop were organized by the Sitterwerk (Katalin Deér, Felix Lehner, Julia Lütolf, Ulrich Meinherz, Ariane Roth, Marina Schütz, Ulrich Vogt), Anthon Astrom and Lukas Zimmer (Astrom/Zimmer), Fabian Wegmüller, and Christian Kern (InfoMedis AG), with additional help from Susanne Bieri, Annette Spiro, and Gerhard Matter.

Archive der Zukunft
Editing: Ariane Roth & Marina Schütz
Photography: Katalin Deér
Design: István Scheibler
Lithography: Henrik Strömberg
Copyediting/Proofreading: Librico Verlagsbüro, Claudia Kühne

www.sitterwerk.ch
www.sitterwerk-katalog.ch